NEW APPROACHES TO EIGHTEENTH-CENTURY LITERATURE

New Approaches to Eighteenth-Century Literature

✎ SELECTED PAPERS FROM THE
ENGLISH INSTITUTE

✎ EDITED WITH A FOREWORD
BY PHILLIP HARTH

COLUMBIA UNIVERSITY PRESS · NEW YORK AND LONDON

1974

LIBRARY OF CONGRESS CATALOGING IN PUBLICATION DATA

ENGLISH INSTITUTE.
NEW APPROACHES TO EIGHTEENTH-CENTURY LITERATURE.

ESSAYS PRESENTED AT TWO CONFERENCES OF THE ENGLISH
INSTITUTE HELD IN 1972 AND 1973.
INCLUDES BIBLIOGRAPHICAL REFERENCES.
1. ENGLISH LITERATURE—18TH CENTURY—ADDRESSES,
ESSAYS, LECTURES.   1. HARTH, JOHN PHILLIP, 1926–   ED.
II. TITLE.
PR553.E5 1974   820'.9'005   74–13808
ISBN 0–231–03928–X

The following essays were presented at two conferences of the English Institute on "New Approaches to Eighteenth-Century Literature," the first in 1972, directed by the editor, the second in 1973, conducted by Lawrence Lipking. The speakers were free to interpret the title of the conferences as they saw fit, with the result that the essays collected here reflect two rather different conceptions of the term "new approaches."

In one sense, the title refers to new directions in the study of eighteenth-century literature, a process of change which is constantly going on in any live discipline. James L. Clifford, commenting a few years ago on the "major trends and current enthusiasms" he had detected in eighteenth-century studies over the preceding quarter of a century, observed that "approaches vary; manners change; there are fascinating shifts of taste; fads have a way of waxing and waning." These changes in the course of criticism come about for a variety of reasons: fluctuations in the popularity of certain authors and genres, shifting emphases on various aspects of the literary work itself, the search for answers to new questions. In an effort to gain some perspective on where the new trends may be leading, Mr. Lipking in his essay identifies the major thrust of eighteenth-century studies in the recent past, predicts several different directions they are likely to take in the near future, and offers some cautionary words on the spirit in which they ought to be carried out. Leo Braudy's essay exemplifies one of the most important new directions in criticism today by turning from the formalist criticism of Richardson's *Clarissa* which has been popular in recent years to consider the attitudes toward personal identity and relations with other people in that novel and to explore social and cultural changes in the eighteenth century which help to explain the presence of these attitudes in *Clarissa*.

To the extent that new directions in literary study reflect the development of fresh interests, such trends can bring greater breadth to the pursuit of criticism from which we all profit. There is another respect, however, in which new approaches result not from asking different questions about literature but from seeking better answers, and in which new trends do not mark a change in direction so much as they indicate a search for greater exactitude. "Why," asked the man whom Johnson called the father of English criticism, "should there be any *ipse dixit* in our poetry, any more than there is in our philosophy?" Dryden was speaking on that occasion of the practice of poetry, but he also applied the same skepticism to the criticism of poetry and in this respect initiated a valuable tradition for his successors. If criticism is to remain a healthy discipline, it must always be ready not only to ask new questions about literature but to seek to find out whether we have been answering familiar questions in the right way. Are the assumptions underlying this criticism trustworthy? Is the method of investigation appropriate in this case? Are the means of interpreting the literature of another period applicable to this particular work? When doubts like these are raised about our critical complacencies, the result in some cases may be new approaches to literature which pursue familiar lines of inquiry, but with greater rigor and more satisfying results.

The remaining essays in this collection are all concerned with new approaches to eighteenth-century literature in this second, more skeptical, sense. Donald Greene begins his essay by tracing the checkered career of eighteenth-century studies, points out their shortcomings as well as their successes, and suggests more accurate approaches to problems which continue to occupy the attention of many critics and scholars as in the past. Some of these new approaches, he indicates, are already being implemented and have led to major revisions in the interpretation of eighteenth-century literature, but the results of this revolution have been slow in displacing older and still popular images of that literature. Ralph Cohen challenges the view, frequently repeated by literary historians, that for eighteenth-century writers and critics the genres were distinct literary forms, each with its own specific effect. In an essay with important implications for the literary history of this period, he argues that much of its best creative and critical writing depended on a theory of the interrelation of forms which in practice led to the creation of mixed genres, as he shows by examining some familiar eighteenth-century works.

Ralph W. Rader also is concerned with genres in his essay, but from the point of view of criticism rather than of literary history, and in a quite different sense of the term. As he points out, he is using genre not "in the prescriptive and conventional sense" specially associated with literary theory and practice in the eighteenth century itself, but in the sense of "the significant representational structures" which eighteenth-century writers actually produced. Opposing the tendency of the New Criticism to conceive all poetry, indeed all literary structures whatever, in terms of a monogeneric poetics of statement, he argues that it is our intuitive understanding of the generic intention of the author that governs our interpretation of a work, even to the meaning of the individual sentences, and he illustrates his thesis by analyzing various eighteenth-century writings. Irvin Ehrenpreis also challenges a favorite belief of the New Critics, the principle of organic form which has led to an emphasis on the implicit meaning of literary works with a corresponding "flight from explicit meaning." Without denying that this principle may be valid for many twentieth-century writings, he vigorously rejects the notion that it is applicable to all literature and argues in particular that it is an inappropriate way of approaching eighteenth-century literature, as he illustrates by examining the lengths to which it has led a number of recent critics in interpreting works of that period.

PHILLIP HARTH

University of Wisconsin, Madison
February, 1974

CONTENTS

X   CONTENTS

NEW APPROACHES TO EIGHTEENTH-CENTURY
LITERATURE

DONALD GREENE

The Study of Eighteenth-Century Literature:

PAST, PRESENT, AND FUTURE

THE past of the academic study of English literature generally is not a heritage whose contemplation can afford much pleasure. It was instituted a little over a century ago, to cater to those unable or unwilling to undertake the more demanding traditional curricula in classics or mathematics. At Oxford in the 1920's, an acute observer—Evelyn Waugh, conceivably the finest novelist, certainly the most brilliant English prose stylist, of his generation—wrote, "English literature was for women and foreigners." In his novel *Brideshead Revisited* the hero is counselled by an older Oxonian, "You're reading History? A perfectly respectable school. The very worst is English Literature." [1]

In American, colonial, Scottish, and redbrick universities, the subject was used to inculcate Victorian morality in middle-class youth. The Reverend Thomas Dale, of University College,

---

[1] Waugh, *A Little Learning* (London, 1964), p. 173; *Brideshead Revisited* (Boston, 1945), p. 26.

London, ancestor of us all as the first holder of the title Professor of English Literature—sobering thought—assured his pupils'
parents, "The gems with which it [English literature] is so co-
piously adorned sometimes require to be abstracted and exhi-
bited with a careful hand, lest they convey pollution with the
foul mass of daring profaneness or disgusting wantonness in
which they are too often encrusted. Never," Dale continued,
"never will I suffer the eye of inexperienced youth to be dazzled
by the brilliancy of genius, when its broad lustre obscures the
deformity of vice." It was Dale who angrily thrust his pupil
John Ruskin's appreciative essay on Byron deep into the entrails
of his desk, not to be disinterred until after his death, and presented Chaucer and other older writers in such a way (Ruskin
reported) that "the laugh of the hearer is generally at, not with,
the author." [2] How the abstracting recommended by Dale was
to be done is demonstrated by the canny William Minto, Professor of Logic [!] and English Literature at the University of Aber-
deen, who advised his students, when they came to Book II of
The Dunciad, "Much of this you had better skip." Although at
times Minto is surprisingly appreciative of Pope as a poetic
craftsman, he does not mention his "Satires"; and, though one is
used to the Victorian conviction that Swift was insane, one is a
little taken aback to find Minto commenting, "The Epistle to
Arbuthnot, I believe, really represents his permanent attitude of
mind, the stable condition in which his mind rested when it had
recovered from any passing derangement of its equilibrium."

[2] D. J. Palmer, *The Rise of English Studies* (London, 1965), pp. 20, 23.
The story about Ruskin's essay is also told in R. W. Chambers, "Philol-
ogists at University College, London," in his *Man's Unconquerable Mind*
(London, 1939).

Swift himself is nowhere mentioned in Minto's lectures, published as *The Literature of the Georgian Era*.[3]

At the more urbane establishments, the pioneer professors of English literature were gentlemanly journalists. At Cambridge there was Sir Arthur Quiller-Couch, author of forgotten third-rate novels, occasionally stooping from his eminence to rebuke uncouth intruders like T. S. Eliot and I. A. Richards.[4] There was Sir Walter Raleigh at Oxford, whose classic description by Virginia Woolf every young instructor should memorize: "He joked, he told stories. He made the undergraduates rock with laughter. He drew them in crowds to his lecture rooms. And they went away loving—something or other. Perhaps it was Keats. Perhaps it was the British Empire. Certainly it was Walter Raleigh. But we should be much surprised if anybody went away loving poetry, loving the art of letters." [5] There was Saintsbury, moved to greater ecstasy, in later life at least, by a vintage burgundy than by literature. True, there were aca-

[3] Port Washington, N. Y., 1970, pp. 70, 68 (first published 1894). Henry Knight Miller's excellent "The Whig Interpretation of Literary History," *Eighteenth-Century Studies*, 6 (Fall 1972), 60–84, which covers some of the same ground this paper does, points out that Thomas Sergeant Perry of Harvard, in his *English Literature in the Eighteenth Century* (1883), likewise omits any mention of *Gulliver's Travels*.

[4] See *Q Anthology*, ed. F. Brittain (London, 1948), pp. 334–51, 409–16.

[5] Virginia Woolf, *Collected Essays*, ed. Leonard Woolf (London, 1969), I, 316. The data of original publication are not given, but the essay is apparently a review of Raleigh's *Letters* (1928). Q. D. Leavis, "The Discipline of Letters: A Sociological Note," *A Selection from Scrutiny*, ed. F. R. Leavis (Cambridge, 1968, I, 7–22; originally appeared in *Scrutiny*, 1945) is equally caustic on Raleigh's protégé and successor (1922) as Merton Professor of English Literature, George Gordon.

demics in the early twentieth century who took literature seriously—Grierson, say, and Ker; on this side of the Atlantic, Kittredge, Lowes, Spingarn; and it is their tradition that our generation has for the most part tried to follow. But in Britain especially, where Q retained his chair until the 1940's and where men like Gosse [6] and Squire, routinely knighted, ruled the interlocking world of literary journalism, the influence of what they stood for remained great, and through the same literary journalism, still persists. That world and its history are described with amusing acerbity by John Gross in *The Rise and Fall of the Man of Letters*, [7] and its academic manifestations with solemnity by D. J. Palmer in *The Rise of English Studies*. With traditional English loftiness, Palmer discusses only England (with a glance at Scotland). That "English studies" may simultaneously, or even earlier, have been "rising" in other parts of the world either does not occur to him or does not interest him. The history of the academic study of English literature in the United States, Australia, Canada, New Zealand, and other English-speaking countries by no means exactly parallels, or derives from, that in Britain. It might be argued, indeed, that differences in that history have resulted (for all that is said in the present paper) in that study—parts of it, at least—now being in a somewhat healthier state in America than in Britain. However that may be, Palmer's book needs to be supplemented by a companion volume on the rise of English studies in other parts of the world in the nineteenth and early twentieth centuries.

[6] Of Gosse, his young cousin Evelyn Waugh wrote, "To me he epitomised all that I found ignoble in the profession of letters" (*A Little Learning*, p. 65). Through his father, Arthur Waugh, who managed the publishing firm of Chapman and Hall, young Waugh was intimately acquainted with the literary "establishment" of London in the 1920's.

[7] New York, 1969.

In the hands of dilettantes and backwoods moralists, the writings of Dryden, Swift, and Pope, addressed to mature and thoughtful adults, got short shrift in Victorian times. At Oxford in 1859, John Richard Green proclaimed, "We instinctively feel the great, the immeasurable distance that severs this age, so proud of its truth, its earnestness, its energy, its high and noble aims, from the heartlessness, the indifference, the frivolity, in one word, the utter worldliness of the eighteenth century" [8]— surely an all-time high in Pharisaism. Emphasizing the inferiority of the eighteenth century to themselves has remained wildly popular with its later students, for obvious psychological reasons. Who were mere teachers of the parvenu subject of English literature to argue this point with so eminent and popular a historian as Green? The words of Henry Reed, Professor of Rhetoric and English Literature in the University of Pennsylvania, find an echo in innumerable student manuals of the time: "Let us now rapidly consider some of the causes, or at least accompaniments, of the degeneracy of English literature, and particularly of its poetry, which began in the latter part of the seventeenth century." He gives a hair-raising account of the "debauchery, licentiousness, riot, and blasphemy" which took place after 1660, and sums it up, "To a nation thus diseased there was perpetually passing the moral poison that issued from the avenues of the palace." Pope's reprehensible morals are responsible for his failure as a poet: when he "exhorts a female friend, 'Not to quit the free innocence of life / For the dull glory of a virtuous wife,' " Reed ejaculates, "What a line for a poet to utter! And what a contrast to those bright images of womanly heroism and beauty which the older poets delighted to picture in

[8] *Studies in Oxford History, Chiefly in the Eighteenth Century* (Oxford, 1901), p. 28.

marriage!" [9] Such as Shakespeare's Goneril and Regan and Milton's Dalila?

On the way such works came into existence, J. Macmillan Brown, of Canterbury College, New Zealand, in the preface to his *Manual of English Literature, 1750–1850* (1894), is illuminating: "The addition of Anglo-Saxon and Early English to the work in English for the pass degree at the University of New Zealand has necessitated the writing of this manual." Brown has to spend so much time lecturing on these new subjects, he tells us, that he has had to make available to his students in print what he had previously delivered to them in lectures concerning more recent literature. He complains pathetically, "I have had to spend my long vacation in attempting a manual that would supply the deficiency."

Understandably, the pedagogy of English literature, hastily devised by the textbook writers of the mid-nineteenth century to meet the sudden demand, relieved the student from the necessity of much deleterious contact with what Swift and the rest actually wrote. That pedagogy consisted of two main techniques, aimed at providing students with neat "facts" to be memorized that they could regurgitate in examinations—what else could "teaching" English literature possibly consist in? First, the long continuum of English literature had to be broken down into manageable "periods" of a century or so. Second, "characteristics" of each "period" had to be formulated, for the student to learn. After that, if there were any time left, some actual reading might take place of selections from the writings of the time, carefully chosen for their "characteristic" quality.

Esther J. Trimble, Professor of Literature in the State Normal School, West Chester, Pennsylvania, in her *Handbook of En-*

---

[9] *Lectures on English Literature* (Philadelphia, 1855), pp. 219, 234.

glish and American Literature for the Use of Schools and Academies,
explains the rationale: "One of the most important lessons that
. . . the genuine student learns is that of sifting. It is impossible
to remember everything, but it is of the utmost importance to
learn to generalize, to take in as nearly as possible the general
and predominant features of a subject, and leaving details for a
more thorough and minute examination. . . . The work is divided into seventeen chapters, each chapter representing an era.
. . . The prominent features of each era could be given in one
lesson, enabling the pupil to get through the outline of the subject [presumably the whole of English and American literature]
in a few lessons." [10] For each of her seventeen eras, Miss Trimble provides a neat list of "points" to be absorbed in the process
of "getting through the outline." Those for the Restoration include such items as "The prevailing taste in literature was low"
and "This age sought methods, rules"—Miss Trimble here is really calling the kettle black. After memorizing these, what student, coming to Miss Trimble's selections from Restoration literature, would dare to find anything there but her "points"? As
the result of this methodology, the familiar labels came into
being—"Neoclassicism" and "Preromanticism," "The Age of
Reason," more recently the fashionable "Augustanism."

If the study of English literature generally was thought the
appropriate subject for "women and foreigners," to whom was
the lowly study of *eighteenth-century* English literature to be con-
signed? Obviously to students of sturdy morality, unlikely to be
so dazzled by the brilliancy of genius as to fall victim to the de-

[10] Philadelphia, 1883, pp. iii–iv. Miss Trimble is only one of dozens
of similar industrious academic hacks in all parts of the English-speaking world who, from the 1840's on, churned out similar manuals. I have
picked her largely at random; many others are listed in H. K. Miller's
"Whig Interpretation" (see n. 3 above).

formity of vice, and to students not too bright or imaginative, qualities wasted on an unimaginative literature—those having them would be guided toward the more rewarding Romantics or Elizabethans: conscientious plodders who could usefully spend their careers cataloguing and labelling the minor and safer writers of the period without danger to their immortal souls. I fear something of this tradition, like others from the nineteenth century, still persists in modern academia.

But let us be optimistic and define "the past" I have been describing as lasting from 1850 or so only to the 1920's, and call the 1920's to 1970's "the present." Certainly much has taken place in eighteenth-century literary study in those decades that deserves applause. We have begun to be provided with the essential tools for the serious study of the important writers of the century. Excellent editions of the works of many of the great writers have appeared; others are in progress or on the drawing board. It has been a period distinguished for biography and the editing of letters, journals, and other biographical material, adhering to standards of accuracy inconceivable a century ago. We have many bibliographical aids not available earlier, though the immense project of an eighteenth-century *Short Title Catalogue* is only beginning to be planned. New and cheap methods of photoreproduction, as well as the burgeoning and not so cheap facsimile reprint industry, have made rare materials accessible to a degree undreamed of when I began serious graduate work twenty years ago. The growing use of computers not only has made possible the production of more, and more competent, concordances to the important writings of the century, but seems to foreshadow exciting new possibilities for the study of style and for the many vexed questions of attribution in the period. This groundwork is still far from complete; but it is not too early to begin to reflect, "Now that we have been given the tools, it is up to us to finish the job." But just what *is* the job?

Some answers to that question began to emerge in the decades I have arbitrarily called "the present." During that time the name of one individual stands out as having done more than anyone else to transform the study of English literature, including that of the eighteenth century, from a subject suitable for "women and foreigners," for pretty, forgettable essays in the *London Mercury*, or for the carefully censored pre-examination notebooks of Professors Dale's and Trimble's pupils—to transform it into what it should be, a study worthy the attention of serious, intelligent, experienced, grown-up men and women, capable of affording them profound and complex aesthetic delight and valuable instruction in the most serious matters of the human condition. I am speaking of T. S. Eliot. Not that all of Eliot's ministrations to eighteenth-century literary study were useful. His "dissociation of sensibility," which he seems later to have repudiated, though students still go on parroting it, and his comments on Swift were only elegant variations of erroneous Victorian stereotypes. Nevertheless, more than one older scholar has commented that the "new era" in eighteenth-century literary study began with Eliot's *Times Literary Supplement* review of Mark Van Doren's book on Dryden's poetry, originally Van Doren's Columbia doctoral dissertation, a review which expanded in 1924 into *Homage to John Dryden*. How astounding— what a far cry from Miss Trimble's dismissal of the whole of the Restoration period, emphatically including Dryden, as representing a "low taste" in literature—to find the most daring avant-garde poet and critic of the day insisting that Dryden was a great poet and that his poetry had much of current importance to say to the modern world! Potentially even more far-reaching

10
DONALD GREENEin its consequences was Eliot's 1930 essay on Johnson's poetry (and on eighteenth-century poetry generally),[11] which with magisterial competence destroys the crippling myth subscribed to by Matthew Arnold and others (first given wide currency by Joseph Warton in his *Essay on the Writings and Genius of Pope*, 1756) that poetry is written in a different language from that of prose—a myth that made it possible for generations of textbook writers to dismiss, or at best patronize, the poetry of Pope, Dryden, Johnson, Goldsmith, Swift, and the rest as "poetry of statement" or "poetry of logical structure," wholly different in kind (and, by implication, inferior in value) to the "suggestive," "imaginative," "unlogical" poetry of earlier and later times.

And it was impossible to brush Eliot aside: clearly, the patrician Eliot, sometime student at Harvard, Oxford, and the Sorbonne, was far more learned, in half a dozen literatures and disciplines, than Miss Trimble, or, for that matter, Q and Raleigh. It was not the pure academics, for all they contributed in the way of editorial, biographical, and bibliographical foundations, who, in the 1920's to '40's animated the study of the literature of the eighteenth century, made it "alive and life-giving"—to quote F. R. Leavis' characterization of Johnson's criticism—but contemporary poets and critics, unattached, or attached somewhat tenuously, to the academic establishment. It must have been a shock to the Dales and Trimbles to find the most eminent poets and critics of the day, Eliot, Leavis, Edmund Wilson, Allen Tate, Yvor Winters, to mention some, acclaiming Samuel Johnson, scorned by the academic textbooks, as a fine poet and one of the greatest critics of all time. "A great critic is the rarest of all literary geniuses; perhaps the only critic in En-

[11] Introduction to *London: A Poem and The Vanity of Human Wishes* (London, 1930); rpt. in *English Critical Essays: Twentieth Century*, ed. Phyllis M. Jones (London, 1933) and elsewhere.

glish who deserves that epithet is Samuel Johnson," wrote Yvor Winters in 1943.[12] At the same time, incredibly, the standard academic view being taught to college students was the following: "In Dr. Samuel Johnson, one of the more favorable examples of what the eighteenth century could do in the development of personality, no one can fail to see the results of this dwindling. Painting, sculpture, architecture, dancing, and acting he cared little for. Music he defined [where, one wonders] as the least unpleasant form of noise. About most of what we refer to by the word 'nature' he knew little and cared less. To that health, beauty, strength, and skill of the body which the wiser ancients had thought to be almost the highest good he did not even aspire. He was gross in appearance and in physical habits. He was often boorish in manners. . . . He did his best literary work in the field of criticism, and even there his judgments were often shaped not by true literary standards but by a dogmatic morality." [13]

To the propagators of such judgments that the eighteenth century represented a lamentable "dwindling" from true artistry, it must have come as a surprise to find Edith Sitwell writing a book (not a very good one, to be sure) in ecstatic praise of Pope, and Auden in some of his most serious poetry introducing long Popean catalogues of personifications, a figure written off by the same textbooks as obsolete and absurd; William Empson exploring the complexly ironic depths of *The Beggar's Opera* (and Brecht using it as the model for his most popular satire of contemporary life), and Cleanth Brooks discovering that the subject of *The Rape*

[12] *The Anatomy of Nonsense* (Denver, 1943), p. 240.
[13] *The College Survey of English Literature*, ed. B. J. Whiting, Fred B. Millett, Alexander M. Witherspoon, Odell Shephard, Arthur Palmer Hudson, Edward Wagenknecht, and Louis Untermeyer (New York, 1942), 1, 781, 779, quoted by H. K. Miller (see n. 3 above).

of the Lock is, after all, rape. Very probably credit should also be
given to Yeats, with his praise of Swift, Berkeley, Goldsmith,
and Burke, and Virginia Woolf's and Lytton Strachey's lively
and perceptive essays on eighteenth-century writers, some of
which appeared early in the century and may have helped to
stimulate the young Eliot's interest in the period. Strachey's
brilliant vindication of Racine, in his *Landmarks in French Literature* (1912), certainly has applications to eighteenth-century English literature. It was around the same time, and probably not
without related significance, that British academic philosophy
began to abjure its late-nineteenth-century flirtation with Hege-
lianism and, under Bertrand Russell, Ayer, and Ryle, returned
to its traditional basis of eighteenth-century British empiricism;
that eighteenth-century music, now heard everywhere, thanks
to the long-playing record, began to be performed and listened
to again; that Victorian pseudo-Gothic architecture began to be
abandoned, and the baroque splendors of Wren, Vanbrugh, and
Hawksmoor began again to be appreciated.

What have we in the academic world done to reinforce and
build on this impressive affirmation by some of the most lively
minds of the first half of the twentieth century that eighteenth-
century literature continues to be highly relevant? (I shall be
using that word again, I'm afraid.) Something, to be sure; not so
much as what might have been done, and what, if we want to,
can still be done. I should like here to consider some features of
the literary scholarship of the last few decades that seem to me
advances, but often imperfectly sustained advances, susceptible
of improvement, and to make suggestions about the directions
we should take in the future if we want to improve them. I mentioned bibliography: the inauguration in 1925 of *Philological
Quarterly's* annual bibliography of English literature, 1660 to
1800, was a landmark not only in bibliography but in raising the

standard set for literary scholarship. Its founder, R. S. Crane, broadened its scope to take in important publications in many other areas, history, philosophy, the fine arts, literatures in other languages. By doing so, he affirmed what I fear some of the present generation of scholars would like to forget, that the study of literature is not a *hortus conclusus* into which one can comfortably retreat and spend one's life playing harmless little self-contained games, ignoring the noisy world outside of on-going scholarship in history, philosophy, theology, and the other humanistic disciplines. As well, Crane used it as a laboratory table on which his scalpel dissected dozens of ill-conceived, ill-argued publications, often portentous Continental dissertations on *le préromanticisme* or *der Neuklassizismus,* and demonstrated their hollowness. The bibliography survives and flourishes, and is even expanding its interdisciplinary content; the Crane standard of criticism less so. We need more Cranes who will say, when the occasion arises—and occasions continue to arise— "This is a dishonest book. It argues *a priori.* It begs the question. It reasons in a circle. It suppresses its middles. It fakes its evidence. It proposes self-fulfilling hypotheses."

The 1920's to '70's too saw the development of the discipline which calls itself the history of ideas. Though its conclusions are now in doubt, I recall the thrill with which I first encountered Louis Bredvold's *The Intellectual Milieu of John Dryden* (1934). Here was a work which seemed to insist that Dryden's poems were not merely something called "literature" and therefore without relevance to what ordinary people did and thought and felt, but rather that they were in the hot center of controversies that people took as seriously and fought over as bitterly as they did over "fascism" and "communism" in the 1930's. Moreover, thanks to Bredvold's lucid exposition, one could see why they thought them important—indeed, why they *were* important.

Marjorie Nicolson, on the impact of the new Newtonian physics on the poetic imagination, gave the same feeling of immediacy. Dryden's and Thomson's poems were not dead museum pieces, graceful artefacts to be viewed "appreciatively," and then forgotten. As much as Auden's and Eliot's they were the records of living minds struggling to cope with living problems. To a backwoods undergraduate, taught by latter-day Dales and Trimbles, the experience was apocalyptic.

Yet many such pioneering works, great as their propaedeutic value was, suffered, we now can see, from a radical flaw. They erected too broad generalizations on too little evidence.[14] I cannot do better than to quote Phillip Harth's remarks in the preface to his book on Dryden that thoughtfully demolished Bredvold's. Professor Harth carefully dissociates what he is doing from "history of ideas." He writes, "I have been . . . concerned in this study with restoring [Dryden's] religious ideas to . . . the historical circumstances in which Dryden conceived and expressed them. This book is in no sense what a well-meaning but mistaken reviewer described an earlier study of mine as being: 'a history-of-ideas exercise in the Basil Willey tradition.' I have made no attempt to construct a single seventeenth-century background, or intellectual milieu, or world picture," and he repudiates the intention of approaching "the problem in a manner popularly associated with the 'history of ideas,' beginning with contemporary 'climates of opinion' and attempting to show how these affected Dryden's thought."[15] Stated thus clearly, it is

[14] From this censure, A. O. Lovejoy's *The Great Chain of Being* must be excepted. Yet in spite of Lovejoy's care never to go beyond his evidence, some eighteenth-century students seem to have acquired the notion that nearly everyone in the century was a believer in the Great Chain. There is no warrant in Lovejoy's book for this. He very properly gives Samuel Johnson credit for its demolition.

[15] Phillip Harth, *Contexts of Dryden's Thought* (Chicago, 1968), pp. viii–ix.

easy to see what the flaw is—apriorism, Miss Trimble's insistence on starting with a big generalization, a "climate of opinion," and then fitting your author into it.

To recommend that we abandon the "history of ideas" approach is not to say that we should stop trying to do what Bredvold and Willey were trying to do—to find out what Dryden and Swift and Pope and their audiences actually thought about certain important matters, what the sources of that thought were, and how that thought can be made intelligible to their modern readers. Rather, it is to recommend that we do even more of it and do it better. The "world picture" method—the bland assumption that we can extrapolate to Dryden or Swift or Johnson what a fairly large number of their lesser contemporaries were allegedly thinking—is the lazy man's: it saves one the chore of reading the numerous books that Dryden and Swift and Johnson read which may have influenced their thinking on various subjects; very often, I'm afraid, it saves some students the labor of reading what Dryden or Swift or Johnson himself has written, or at any rate of reading it with close attention and without preconceptions.

And of course one cannot get far into the sense of a great deal that Dryden, Swift, Defoe, and the rest wrote without a certain competence in other disciplines—in political, social, and economic history, in theology and church history, in philosophy and aesthetics, sometimes in art and architecture, in classical, Renaissance Latin, French, or Italian literature. It is appalling how readily literary scholars pronounce on such matters with perhaps no better equipment than what information they may have picked up in a freshman survey course, which even then may have been several decades out of date. The picture of the political scene in eighteenth-century Britain that they acquired from high-school textbooks or Victorian histories—the neat dichotomy of forward-looking Whigs and backward-looking Tories—

was demolished forty years ago by Namier, but goes on being
repeated in innumerable literary surveys. One still encounters
the innocent acceptance of the Weber-Tawney thesis, that modern capitalism was a by-product of Protestantism, as though it
were undisputed fact. Yet one can pick up a modern popular
survey of theological scholarship and read, "There have been
perhaps three major developments in the study of sixteenth-century church history since 1930: first, the destruction of the orthodoxy about 'religion and the rise of capitalism' . . . both
theories [Weber's and Tawney's] were rendered almost untena-
ble by K. Samuelsson in *Religion and Economic Action.*" [16] The
distinguished Renaissance historian, Geoffrey Elton, confessing
that, in spite of its long-lasting "orthodoxy," he, for one, was
"never able to see any real sense" in the Weber-Tawney contention, entirely concurs. "It was not Calvinism," he concludes
after summarizing Samuelsson's careful compilation of historical
data bearing on the matter, "that freed man from the restraints
of the traditional moral concepts in economics, but emancipation
from religion and theology in general." [17]

When it comes to matters of religious doctrine and ecclesias-
tical history, the flounderings of literary scholars professing to
explicate the Christian beliefs of Swift and Fielding and Johnson
pass credence. If someone who sets out to pronounce on such

[16] Jean [Cardinal] Daniélou, A. H. Couratin, and John Kent, in *The
Pelican Guide to Modern Theology* (Harmondsworth, 1969–70), II (*Historical Theology*), 271. Kurt Samuelsson, an economic historian, published
his work in Swedish (*Ekonomi och Religion*) in 1957; the English translation by E. Geoffrey French was published in 1961 (London). To show
the extent of Weber's influence, Samuelsson quotes (p. 8, 1961 ed.) a
passage from Wellek and Warren's *Theory of Literature* (1955) in
praise of him.

[17] *Reformation Europe 1517–1559* (Cleveland & New York, 1964), p.
317.

matters cannot bring himself to study the works of South and Hammond and Pearson and the other Anglican divines whom Swift and Fielding and Johnson studied, or a competent modern handbook of orthodox Christian theology, he might at the very least try to gain some familiarity with the Thirty-Nine Articles of Religion of the Church of England. If scholars would absorb even Articles IX to XI, which occupy less than a page in the average Prayer Book, and would recall that Swift and Fielding and Johnson subscribed to those Articles, we might hear less fantasy about their Pelagianism or semi-Pelagianism or latitudinarianism—defined in literary scholarship, but nowhere else, as a kind of Pelagianism. The recent standard biography of a somewhat important eighteenth-century poet who wrote much on religious themes speculates whether or not he may at some time or other have been ordained as a clergyman of the Church of England. It goes on to speculate that, though there is no clear evidence of his having received ordination as a deacon or priest, he may possibly have taken "minor orders"—as though the Church of England, like the Roman Catholic church, possessed such orders! There are studies of the religion of eighteenth-century English writers which quote in evidence excerpts from the 1789 Prayer Book of the Episcopal Church of America, unaware of its substantial differences from the English 1662 Book of Common Prayer. And so on.

It is astonishing how naively scholars accept as gospel the current line of opposition propaganda which Swift and Pope made fine literature of—about, say, the hostility of Walpole and the first two Georges to the arts and learning. Shakespeare's *Richard III* too is fine literature, but a modern critic who accepted it as the definitive account of English political history of the late fifteenth century would have it gently suggested to him that he should consult a psychiatrist. Has a single Pope scholar ever suggested, in print, that Pope's propaganda, in the *Epistle to Burlington*, for the Palladian revival in architecture as against the earlier baroque of Wren, Vanbrugh, and Hawksmoor, is, after all, propaganda, and cautioned the student that the "false taste" against which Pope inveighs is regarded by most modern art critics as possessing much greater artistic merit than the works of the neo-Palladians? The closest thing to a protest I have seen has been a footnote by F. W. Bateson in the Twickenham edition, on line 20, where Bateson comments apropos of Bubb Dodington's house at Eastbury: "The architect was Vanbrugh, for whose abilities Pope shared Swift's ignorant contempt." *Si sic omnia dixisset!* In fact, of course, Walpole's country seat, Houghton Hall, which he commissioned Colin Campbell to design, is a magnificent piece of architecture, and housed one of the greatest art collections of the time (after his death, it was bought by Catherine the Great and became the nucleus of the Hermitage collection). The greatest music ever composed in England was produced under the patronage of George I and George II, by their protégé Handel. George I founded the Regius Professorships of Modern History at Oxford and Cambridge, and George II chartered two important educational institutions in his dominions, King's College, now Columbia University, in New York, and the University of Göttingen, whose library was the wonder of the eighteenth-century academic world because of the unprecedentedly generous governmental funding it received. The government of Walpole and Newcastle was no more "corrupt" than most governments at most times. The "garden" part of Maynard Mack's recent monograph on Pope, *The Garden and the City*, is a superb piece of work, but the "city" section, dealing with the contemporary political scene, disappoints by accepting uncritically much of the myth of Walpolian villainy.

I have perhaps said enough to suggest that one crying need for the future of eighteenth-century English literary study is for its practitioners to resolve to try to keep up with current scholarship in the other areas of eighteenth-century cultural and intellectual history which his work overlaps. It seems to me that in the scholarship of the periods before and after ours, fewer such distressing exhibitions occur. No Miltonist or Spenserian would now be permitted to publish work displaying such blatant ignorance of theology as some of that published on Swift, no Carlylean or Ruskinian work presenting so perversely erroneous a picture of contemporary political history as some done on Johnson. This is due, at least in part, to the activity of scholarly groups and journals dedicated specifically to improving interdisciplinary knowledge in those periods—the Renaissance Society of America and its *Quarterly*, the journal *Victorian Studies*. A national society, with regional branches and a journal and other publications dedicated to fostering interdisciplinary awareness in eighteenth-century studies, has recently been founded. Perhaps in time it may help to make this aspect of eighteenth-century literary studies somewhat brighter. That at least is its aim, and I hope it is not a breach of decorum for me to recommend its support to you.

Not, of course, that it is only literary scholars who demonstrate obtuseness and faulty scholarship. J. H. Plumb, in his popular handbook, *England in the Eighteenth Century* (1950),[18] much relied on by literary students for "background," gives an account of the Church of England in that century—the old business about sloth, cynicism, self-seeking bishops, and so on—that had been conclusively refuted in the early 1930's by Norman Sykes's classic *Church and State in Eighteenth-Century England*.[19] It is even more astonishing to find an eminent professor of church

[18] Harmondsworth.
[19] Cambridge, 1934; rpt. Hamden, Conn., 1962.

history, G. R. Cragg, following much the same line as late as
1968.[20] "What," I have been asked pathetically, "is the use of
the literary scholar's trying to familiarize himself with other disciplines when you tell us that even such distinguished scholars
in other disciplines as Plumb and Cragg and the writers of the
many historical surveys which propound the Weber-Tawney
thesis are not to be relied on?" The answer, I'm afraid, is a hard
one: you have to familiarize yourself sufficiently with the other
fields to know what *idées reçues* are being challenged—and, moreover, develop your general intellectual critical sense to the point
where you sense that even some of the *idées reçues* in other fields
which have not been challenged ought to be. This program is
not so hard as it might sound. Any student who has advanced to
the point of being able to tell whether a new biography of, say,
Swift, or a new critical study of *Tom Jones*, is a good or a bad
one, should have little difficulty in telling whether the glib, un-
documented generalities of Plumb, Cragg, and the standard
"survey" presentations of Weber-Tawney, on the one hand, or
the careful, sober, heavily documented studies of Sykes and
Samuelsson on the other, are more worthy of a scholar's respect.
Elton on the Weber-Tawney debacle is worth quoting: "The at-
traction of the universalising generalisation has, as so often,
proved too much for the sceptical spirit which alone saves the
historian from falling into the pitfalls dug by his own, very necessary, imagination. In the face of the long and ramifying controversy, sadness is the only feeling: sadness at so much
misguided effort, and sadness at the willingness of historians to
worship the graven images set up by the sociologist." [21] There is
no help for it: the literary student must accustom himself to

[20] See Cragg's essay "The Churchman," in *Man Versus Society in
Eighteenth-Century Britain*, ed. James L. Clifford (Cambridge, 1968).

[21] *Reformation Europe*, p. 318.

close, skeptical examination of the graven images set up by the political or social or intellectual or art historian—men whose disciplines, however, he cannot afford to neglect. However widely the image is worshipped, scholarly feet of clay are not all that hard to detect.

One other discipline was added to the eighteenth-century scholar's repertoire during the mid-twentieth century—that of psychology, or rather one particular school of psychology, that of Freud. Readers of *American Imago* and *Literature and Psychology*, as well as of a number of modern biographies of writers of our period, will be aware how exclusively the doctrines of that school hold sway in the psychological interpretation of literature and literary biography. Psychological analysis may well be capable of providing true and useful insights here, and those who have pioneered its use should be congratulated and encouraged. But again, even more useful results might be forthcoming if scholars would keep up with more recent developments. Freud, after all, has long been dead, and even during his lifetime there were those who were not prepared to grant that no psychological truth can subsist outside the canon of his works. In a useful handbook published in 1961 and often reprinted, J. A. C. Brown's *Freud and the Post-Freudians*,[22] only the first two of its ten chapters expound orthodox Freudianism. Chapter Three is on "The Early Schismatics," Adler, Jung, and the rest; later come three chapters on important post-Freudians, Karen Horney, Erich Fromm, and Harry Stack Sullivan, who largely ignore, and often firmly reject Freud's teachings. The application of their methods to the psychoanalysis of Swift and Johnson might bring more fruitful results than those which explain everything in terms of their orality or anality, and perhaps the fu-

[22] Harmondsworth.

ture will display a greater willingness on the part of literary
scholars to explore these newer approaches.

A very important feature of the period I am calling "the
present" was, of course, the "new criticism," which, since its
methods are almost indistinguishable from those of Johnson,
could as well have been called the "old criticism"—the minute
examination of a literary text, assessing the precise meanings of
its words, the effects of its rhetoric, the tensions and ironies implicit in its collocations of statements and images. The methods
of Brooks and Empson—and Eliot and Mack and Brower, to
mention others—have probably contributed more to the reani-
mation of eighteenth-century literary study than any other. I am
told that "new criticism" is in bad odor at the moment, and I
recently saw F. R. Leavis, who sporadically practiced it, condemned on the grounds that he reads a poem by Pope or Donne
"as though it had been written only yesterday." I am not quite
sure just what, on the whole, is wrong with that. Some illumi-
nation is cast on the problem by the controversy between F. W.
Bateson and Leavis over the reading of the climactic lines of
Book IV of *The Dunciad*, which describe the effects of current
(and later) educational methods on their victims:

> First slave to Words, then vassal to a Name,
> Then dupe to Party; child and man the same;
> Bounded by Nature, narrowed still by Art,
> A trifling head, and a contracted heart.

Leavis had heard here an echo of Marvell's

> Tortur'd, besides each other part,
> In a vain head and double heart,

and spoken of the continuity of the "line of wit" from Marvell to Pope. Bateson would have none of this, maintaining that his superior knowledge of the eighteenth-century intellectual "context" enabled him to pronounce that in the Marvell passage "head" and "heart" are concrete images, "picture language," whereas in the Pope passage, since Pope was an "Augustan," they are "grey abstractions." If, of course, we had been told that the *Dunciad* passage had been written by a "metaphysical" poet, the effect would be quite different. Leavis was understandably amazed at such a contention.[23]

There *is* one important matter arising out of chronology which one hopes the future will make an effort to rectify—though it is not this, I think, that the opponents of "new criticism" have in mind. It is simply that words often meant something different in the eighteenth century from what they do now. One would expect professors of English to be aware of this fact; yet some of the most preposterous of recent contributions to misinterpretation and obfuscation have come from apparent ignorance of it. It has often been pointed out that in the eighteenth century and earlier the word "fond" normally meant, as Johnson's *Dictionary* has it, "Foolish, silly; . . . injudiciously indulgent." Yet only the other day my contention that Swift expected us to admire the Houyhnhnms was triumphantly refuted for about the tenth time by pointing to the statement in *Gulliver's Travels* "They have no fondness for their colts or foals"— how could Swift possibly want us to admire beings who don't love their children! [24] In the latest book by a well-known critic,

[23] The controversy is reprinted in F. R. Leavis, ed., *A Selection from Scrutiny* (Cambridge, 1968), II, 280–316.

[24] Paul C. Davies, in *Eighteenth-Century Studies*, 6 (Spring 1972), 464–66.

the climactic line in *The Vanity of Human Wishes*, "Still raise for
good the supplicating voice," is explicated as a further indication
of Johnson's well-known pessimism: "The 'Still' is powerfully, if
sadly, concessive here in its acknowledgment that we cannot expect to see results." [25] The critic is unaware that "still" can have
any other sense than its modern concessive one: he thinks Johnson is saying, "STILL [anyway, nevertheless], raise for good the
supplicating voice." Some here, at least, have encountered the
word "still" in other sixteenth- to eighteenth-century writing—
"Still to be neat, still to be drest"; "Fighting still, and still destroying"—and know what its normal meaning is—"always,"
"continually." Teachers and handbooks go on telling students
that Johnson's chapter heading in *Rasselas*, "The Dangerous
Prevalence of Imagination," is clear proof of the defectiveness of
Johnson's and the eighteenth century's view of life and literature. Since when we say "Colds are prevalent" we mean that
there are a lot of them, Johnson is saying that there is a
dangerously large amount of imagination floating about and that
it should be reduced. Highly logical; except that Johnson's *Dictionary* defines "prevalence" not as "frequent occurrence" but as
"superiority; predominance." The phrase means "When fantasy
prevails over one's contact with reality, the consequences are
likely to be dangerous," a proposition with which any modern
psychiatrist would agree. This is not nit-picking: in each of
these examples, and others could be added, the misreading of a
simple word in its twentieth- instead of its eighteenth-century

[25] Murray Krieger, *The Classic Vision* (Baltimore, Md., 1971), p. 141.
The section on the eighteenth century in the book is entitled "The Retreat from Extremity Through the Worship of Bloodless Abstractions."
Miss Trimble and others to the contrary notwithstanding, it has never
been demonstrated that eighteenth-century writers were fonder of abstractions, bloodless or bloody, than those of any other century.

sense is used to pervert the meaning of an important literary document from what its author was trying to communicate to the precise opposite. With the *OED* and Johnson's *Dictionary* available in relatively cheap reprint form, there is no excuse for this kind of thing; even Webster's Third New International usefully lists such older significations. In the future, let us consult them, and encourage our students to consult them, oftener when we set out to explicate an eighteenth-century text.

I come at last to the most important, and most difficult, task we have to set ourselves if the study of eighteenth-century English literature is to develop in the future into the fully mature and rewarding discipline it can and should be. That task is the final and complete abandonment of the labelling and compartmentalizing myths that are our heritage from the Miss Trimbles and Edmund Gosses. I and others have been campaigning against them for some time, and I have yet to see any serious counter-argument—any refutation of the following propositions: (1) The century and a half between 1660 and 1800 was *not* "The Age of Reason"; on the contrary, the reputation of reason, in the sense of abstract cerebration, could hardly have been lower. Baconian and Lockean empiricism has conclusively triumphed over Aristotelian and scholastic exaltation of the human *nous*. "Dim as the borrowed beams of moon and stars . . . ," writes Dryden, "is Reason to the soul." Man, Swift insists, is not *animal rationale* but at best, *rationis capax*—and perhaps of not very much, at that. "Reason is, and ought always to be, the slave of the passions," Hume sums up his epistemology. (2) It was *not* "The Age of Neoclassicism": no "revival of interest" in the classics took place in 1660; interest in the classics remained continuous among literate Englishmen from the Renaissance to the early twentieth century, and Swift, Pope, and the rest were no more under their spell than Spenser and Milton before them or Shelley and Matthew Arnold after them—very possibly less. "I will now maintain," wrote C. S. Lewis, "that Shelley is to be regarded . . . a more *classical* poet than Dryden. . . . To any one who still thinks Pope a classical poet we can only say 'Open your Sophocles, your Virgil, your Racine, your Milton'; and if that experiment does not convince him, we may safely dismiss him for a blockhead." [26] (3) It was *not* "the Augustan Age." A diligent search reveals a handful of writers of the time speaking casually of "an Augustan age" in English literature—but it is never the age in which the writer himself lives, always an earlier one. Atterbury, writing in the reign of William III, locates it tentatively in that of Charles II; Goldsmith, writing in the last year of George II's reign, suggests (not very seriously) that it was the reign of Anne. Clearly Atterbury and Goldsmith did not think that *they* were Augustans or living in an Augustan age. Good writers, then as now (and earlier), did not display the complacency about the achievements of themselves and their contemporaries that the label, in this context, suggests. And these rare passages in which "Augustan" is used as a term of approval are heavily outweighed by the numerous places in which other writers of the time, including Dryden, Pope, Swift, and Johnson, speak disparagingly of the despotism of Augustus's regime and the sycophancy of the writers—even Horace and Virgil—whom he patronized.[27] (4) It was *not* "the Enlightenment." That term designates a group of Continental, mostly French, writers whose characteristic animus was anti-revelation

[26] "Shelley, Dryden, and Mr. Eliot," in his *Selected Literary Essays*, ed. Walter Hooper (Cambridge, 1969). The essay was first published in 1956.

[27] See Howard D. Weinbrot, "History, Horace, and Augustus Caesar: Some Implications for Eighteenth-Century Satire," *Eighteenth-Century Studies* (forthcoming).

and anti-clerical. Perhaps two important English writers of the time, Hume and Gibbon, have some distant affinity with them. But to try to fit, say, Dryden, Swift, Defoe, and Johnson into that pattern is absurd. Like the rest of the vast majority of English intellectuals of the time, they were sincere professing Christians. Some, like Swift, could certainly see faults in the Church which they loyally served; but the remedy, for Swift, was emphatically not the "free-thinking" of an Anthony Collins or a Voltaire.

Is all the above, when addressed to so select and knowledgeable an audience as the English Institute, merely a preaching to the converted? Is it not beating a dead horse, knocking down a straw man, kicking at an open door? Do members of this Institute really need to be informed that the old Victorian distortions about "an age of prose and reason," with "stress on order, decorum, control, and rules" have been effectively challenged? Does not the latest full-scale college anthology of eighteenth-century writing, the excellent Tillotson-Fussell-Waingrow volume, begin with the firm assertion, "The English eighteenth century . . . has been called The Enlightenment, The Age of Reason, The Neoclassical Period, and The Augustan Age. But the more closely we attend to the actual writings, the more we perceive that the literature and thought of the period are too varied, surprising, and complex to contain themselves comfortably under any of these labels"? [28] The job of demolition has been thoroughly done; why bore us by continuing to do it over and over?

If what I am now saying presents little or no novelty to the members of the English Institute, I am glad. Yet I think it

[28] *Eighteenth-Century English Literature*, ed. Geoffrey Tillotson, Paul Fussell, and Marshall Waingrow (New York, 1969), p. 1.

should be of concern to the leaders, in America, of the academic study of English literature that not only they, but the thousands of others engaged in what passes for "teaching the eighteenth century" in high schools and colleges, should also become aware of such basic matters. They should be aware, and disturbed, that, whatever may be the case with themselves and their fortunate students, the battle, on these more elementary and widely populated levels, is far from having been won—it has hardly even begun. It is safe to say that the great bulk of those teaching Dryden, Swift, Pope, Johnson and their contemporaries at the high-school or lower-division undergraduate level are not even aware that a battle has been in progress, that the views of Arnold and Gosse and the school textbooks of the 1890's have ever been challenged.

Those who doubt this should skim through the latest batch of poetry anthologies designed for the lucrative college freshman trade—dozens are published every year—and see what happens to eighteenth-century poetry in them. The ghost of Matthew Arnold remains all powerful. Though they will contain large chunks of Allen Ginsberg—and even Eliot and Donne—the eighteenth century will probably be represented by a short excerpt from the *Essay on Man* and little else, with a derogatory commentary such as the following:

There have . . . been periods in the history of poetry which evolved severe and rigid conventions of form. The heroic couplet, lines ten syllables long and riming in pairs, was a required device of anything claiming to be a poem in eighteenth-century England. So these lines [eight lines from the *Essay*, beginning "Know then thyself, presume not God to scan"] would be acceptably "poetic" while "This Is Just To Say" [a piece of free verse by William Carlos Williams, previously quoted] would not make it. It wouldn't make it on the content count either, not being suitably high-minded. A poet in the eighteenth century therefore ran the risk of censorship in form as well as content. If he said anything seamy, they could get him for content; if he didn't use the heroic couplet in saying his seamy thing, they could fault him for form.[29]

It is clear that much elementary education of educators still needs to be done. The first step in that of the author of this preposterous and obsolete nonsense—published for the instruction of the young in the 1970s!—might be to require him to read through the three volumes of the standard edition of Swift's poetry, page by page. And after that Matthew Prior and Christopher Smart and William Cowper, to mention a few.

Or we might ponder this, from a pamphlet published in 1970 with the imprimatur of the National Council of Teachers of English, urging drastic revisions to the traditional curriculum in English literature under the auspices of the blessed word "relevance." Knowing the history of the academic study and teaching of eighteenth-century literature, we might have predicted that it would rank high on the scale of priorities for elimination. And so it turns out: "Another unlikely candidate for their [college students'] attention is eighteenth-century literature. Why require reading in classical literature, with its stress on order, decorum, control and rules, when these are the very states young men and women consciously and unconsciously deplore?" (It is ironic that Minto banned *Dunciad* II from his classroom precisely because of its "seamy" *lack* of decorum.)

The eighteenth-century requirement is very unpopular with undergraduates. Traditionally, we drag them screaming through an anthology or series of Riverside neoclassicists from

[29] Anthony C. Winkler, *Poetry as System* (Glenview, Ill., 1971), pp. 103–04.

Dryden to Johnson, with wistful sidelong glances at Cowper, Collins, Gray, Smart, Young, and others. Too many teachers of the eighteenth century devote themselves principally to matters of repugnance to modern students: influence of Juvenal and Horace on Pope and Johnson; the conservative morality of the period; elaborate discussions of satire and its uses; the metrical genius (the sound and sense) of these masters of the heroic couplet. Professors may find these topics pregnant with value; they certainly feel that students should be "exposed" to these writers. Most students are bored stiff. A young lady once wrote for a professor at Carnegie-Mellon University:

Nothing so true as what you once let fall:
Most English majors don't dig Pope at all.[30]

Reuben Brower and Maynard Mack might as well have never existed—or, for that matter, Eliot and Auden, who "dug" Pope and his "metrical genius" a great deal. In not "digging" him, the young lady and the writer of the pamphlet are demonstrating that their response to poetry has not advanced beyond that of Matthew Arnold and the aesthetic sensibility of the 1880's. It is the incredible obsoleteness of the writer's picture of what the study of eighteenth-century literature involves that astounds one. The ghost of Miss Trimble is still potent; one feels that our young "radical" reformer would have got high marks on her final examination.

The odd thing is that the poetry of an earlier generation, that of Donne and Herbert and Marvell, though equally despised in the nineteenth century by the Trimbles and the Gosses, is now

[30] Barrett John Mandel, *Literature and the English Department* (Chicago, 1970), p. 57.

treated in these same textbooks of the 1970's with the respect it deserves, is not marked down for deletion on grounds of irrelevance to modern youth. Somehow or other what Eliot and others said in the 1920's and 1930's about the metaphysical poets "got through"; what they said at the same time about Dryden and Pope and Johnson, somehow or other, has not. Why this has been so is, in itself, an interesting question in intellectual history, and one that I think members of the English Institute, especially those primarily concerned with the eighteenth century, have a certain responsibility to address themselves to.

I will not speculate here on what I think the answer may be. I don't, however, think the answer is to respond to the charge of "irrelevance," as perhaps some scholars of that literature have been doing, by, in effect, accepting it, even welcoming it, by insisting that the study of literature *is* an arcane task for a few specialists, an end in itself. I was recently scolded vehemently in print for mentioning, in connection with Swift's denunciations of human bloodshed and torture in his own time, that they seemed to apply at least equally to some more recent examples of human bloodshed and torture: somehow or other I had committed an embarrassing breach of scholarly decorum in doing so.[31] I can only say that I continue to believe that few things more relevant to twentieth-century political history have ever been written, or are likely to be, than *Gulliver's Travels*. I think few things have ever been written more relevant to what is said to be the current deterioration in the quality of American life than *The Dunciad*, or to the problem of individual human happiness now or at any other time than *The Vanity of Human Wishes*. If I did not believe these works to be highly relevant to my own life, and that of my students, I should not go on trying to study

[31] See n. 24 above.

and teach them, but would endeavor to find other employment
in some honest trade. There is at least one critic on my side in
this, a man who wrote, in the eighteenth century, "The only
end of writing is to enable the readers better to enjoy life, or
better to endure it." I believe that if teachers and students would
accept this principle; would accept that a good deal of eighteenth-century English literature has this enabling power—that
fine literature of the eighteenth century, like that of others, is, as
Ezra Pound said, news that stays news; would abandon the notion that the only end of reading it is to put it away into an as-
sortment of ingeniously labelled pigeonholes; would dedicate
themselves, by increasing their knowledge of the historical,
theological, and other matters that Dryden, Swift, and the rest
are writing about, and then actually *reading* their writings, with
due attention to semantics and without preconceptions, to
achieving a genuine understanding and appreciation of them;
and, having achieved it, would try to stimulate their students to
do the same, the future of eighteenth-century literary study
could be a reasonably bright one—brighter, at any rate, than the
ominous one foreshadowed in the two quotations from twentieth-century teachers of it that I have given above.

RALPH COHEN

On the Interrelations of Eighteenth-Century Literary Forms

I. THE HISTORICAL BACKGROUND

MODERN critics, in discussing neoclassical genres, have insisted on the rigidity of forms, while acknowledging that eighteenth-century critics disagreed about and poets seemed to diverge from this "rigidity." Austin Warren wrote: "That genres are distinct—and also should be kept distinct—is a general article of Neo-Classical faith. But if we look to Neo-Classical criticism for definition of genre or method of distinguishing genre from genre, we find little consistency or even awareness of the need for a rationale." [1] James Sutherland, in *A Preface to Eighteenth Century Poetry*, declared: "You knew where you were with Pastoral, Elegy, Epic, and the rest; you were not called upon to adjust yourself to the untried or the unexpected. Even in the eighteenth century, however, men were not willing to bask for ever in the traditional perfections. . . . The characteristic compromise was to seek variety within the established form: not to

[1] René Wellek and Austin Warren, *Theory of Literature* (New York, 1949), p. 239.

abandon the known Kinds, but to introduce a slight change of
subject or treatment." [2]

Oliver F. Sigworth wrote that at the center of neoclassic criticism is "the conception of genre, of literary works existing as
species in an absolute sense." "Each genre had its own rules, its
own (to use the proper term) *decorum*, which extended not only
to matters of form and structure—matters which we still
vaguely understand—but also to verse and diction." [3] Emerson
R. Marks declared that for neoclassical critics, "Each poem
shines with its own peculiar beauty; and it more or less followed
from this that the kinds should never be mixed." [4] René Wellek,
in *A History of Modern Criticism*, wrote: "The rules were rarely
defined in general terms but rather specified according to genres.
The distinction between genres was basic to the neoclassical
creed, so basic that its assumptions were never, to my knowledge, properly examined during this time. . . . It was rarely
clear whether the table of genres was closed or whether new
genres could be admitted. In practice hybrids of existing
genres or ruleless new genres outside of the table of categories
arose and were at least tolerated." [5]

These critics posit the distinctiveness of the kinds, although
some treat them as metaphysical absolutes, whereas others find
them governed by rules and decorum. They recognize that al-

[2] London, 1948, 1963, p. 124.

[3] *Criticism and Aesthetics, 1660–1800* (San Francisco, 1971), pp. xv,
xvi.

[4] *The Poetics of Reason* (New York, 1968), p. 92. See also Francis
Gallaway, *Reason, Rule and Revolt in English Classicism* (Lexington, Ky.,
1940), p. 228: "the distaste for any mixture of 'kinds' indicate(s) the
preoccupation of neo-classicists with the Rules of specific literary
forms."

[5] New Haven, 1955, I, 19, 20.

though eighteenth-century critics do not always agree on the
rules or the decorum of specific kinds, they do agree that distinct kinds exist, common responses to which are the result of
shared beliefs in a general human nature. Each kind has its own
specific effect—the single pointedness of epigram, the sweet
communication of loss in elegy, the artful delivery of precepts in
didactic poetry, the moral end of drama. The means by which
the effects were achieved included subject (theme, fable,
thought, sentiments, speaker), language (diction, imagery, rhetorical figures), style (sublime, low, etc.), and meter. Irène
Simon puts it this way: "when approaching any poem the critic
would first ask himself to what genre the work belonged, what
instruction it intended to convey, whether the plot and characters did convey it, whether the design of the poem and the characters were such that nature was imitated all through, whether
the style was suitable to the characters and to the sentiments they
expressed, etc. Any critical examination would therefore consider in turn: the fable, the manners (i.e. the characters), the sentiments, the diction and the metre." [6]
My argument is that these critics are mistaken. They are mistaken in assuming that the distinctiveness of kinds was agreed
upon; they are mistaken in assuming that the rules specified the
kinds; they are mistaken in assuming that each kind was bound
to a clearly defined specific effect. Rather, the poetic kinds were
identified in terms of a hierarchy that may not have been all-
inclusive (since not all possible forms were specified) but were
all interrelated. And this hierarchy can be seen in terms of the
inclusion of lower forms into higher—the epigram into satire,
georgic, epic; the ode into epic; the sonnet into drama; the prov-

[6] *Neo-Classical Criticism 1660–1800*, ed. Irène Simon (Columbia, S. C.,
1971), p. 14.

erb into all preceptive forms. Edward Phillips refers to this hierarchy as "the *Epic*, the *Dramatic*, the *Lyric*, the *Elegiac*, the *Epoenetic*, the *Bucolic*, or the Epigram"—in them "the whole circuit of Poetic design is one way or other included." For Phillips the epigram is the "fag end of Poetry" as epic is "of the largest extent, and includes all that is narrative either of things or persons." [7] Dryden considered epic the top and epigram "the bottom of all poetry." [8] John Sheffield undertakes to rehearse the "differing kinds" of poetry, beginning with song, and moving through elegy, ode, satire and drama to epic, for

Heroick Poems have a just pretence
To be the chief effort of humane sence.[9]

The critics argued that, although each form had its own effect, it was, either in terms of its parts or as a whole, interrelated with other forms. Some types of poems were mixtures to begin with: Dryden pointed out that Varronian satire was a mixture of several sorts of verse and was also mixed with prose; moreover, these poems had various subjects. In praising the proper satire—that of Boileau—he describes it as "The majesty of the heroic, finely mixed with the venom of the other." And he refers to satire as a species of heroic poetry.[10] The georgic poem was a mixture of instruction and story: some lyric forms were closely related to the heroic poem; others to the pastoral or epigram.

[7] "Preface to Theatrum Poetarum (1675)," *Critical Essays of the Seventeenth Century*, ed. J. E. Spingarn (Oxford, 1908–09), II, 266, 267.

[8] Dryden, "A Discourse Concerning the Original and Progress of Satire," *Of Dramatic Poesy and Other Critical Essays*, ed. George Watson (London, 1962), II, 82.

[9] "An Essay Upon Poetry," Spingarn, II, 295.

[10] Dryden, II, 113–15, 149.

Norman Maclean remarks that the divine and heroic odes or lyrics are placed "near the top of the poetical hierarchy (along with epic and tragedy) and the minor lyric near the bottom (generally somewhere between pastoral and epigram)." [11]

The theory of interrelation of forms had been inherited from Renaissance critics such as Minturno, Patrizzi, and others. Sir Philip Sidney had noted in his *Apology:* "Now in his parts, kindes, or *Species* (as you list to terme them), it is to be noted that some Poesies have coupled together two or three kindes, as Tragicall and Comicall, wher-upon is risen the Tragi-comicall. Some in the like manner have mingled Prose and Verse, as *Sanazzar* and *Boetius.* Some have mingled matters Heroicall and Pastorall. But that commeth all to one in this question, for, if severed they be good, the conjunction cannot be hurtfull." [12]

The mingling of different "matters" within the heroic poem was only one of the very many ways in which Renaissance critics saw the forms as interrelated. Rosalie Colie has remarked that in the Renaissance a rigid system of genres "never existed in practice and barely even in theory . . . . We have been looking at far too many examples of works that involve mixed kind rather than a specific single kind to accept any such rule." [13] Late seventeenth-century critics continued to see the forms as interrelated, though their interrelations often differed from those named by Renaissance critics. Hobbes, for example, even when he objected to the "received" hierarchies, did so by suggesting

[11] "From Action to Image: Theories of the Lyric in the Eighteenth Century," *Critics and Criticism*, ed. R. S. Crane (Chicago, 1952), p. 410.

[12] Sidney, "An Apologie for Poetrie," *Elizabethan Critical Essays*, ed. G. Gregory Smith (London [1904] 1950), I, 175. The terms "kindes," "species," "forms," and "genres" are used interchangeably throughout the paper.

[13] Rosalie L. Colie, *The Resources of Kind* (Berkeley, 1973), pp. 114–15.

an extended theory of mixtures. He listed only three "Sorts," "*Heroique, Scommatique* and *Pastorall*," and declared that the forms named by critics—"Sonets, Epigrams, Eclogues, and the like Peeces"—were "but other Essayes and parts of an entire Poem." [14]

Joseph Trapp, professor of poetry at Oxford, wrote that the "Epic Poem . . . comprehends within its Sphere all the other Kinds of Poetry whatever; and is in this Art what the Organ is in Music, which with various Pipes, inflated with the same Breath, charms us not only with its own Harmony, but represents that of every other Instrument." [15] If the epic could include every other kind—satire, pastoral, ode, elegy, panegyric, epigram, etc.—then the epic can be seen, in Trapp's view, as a harmony of forms, and each form can be understood in terms of its interrelation with others, capable of containing, within itself, appropriate parts of others. This decorum, then, is the propriety by which forms can be included in other forms and the propriety by which elements of one form—diction, rhetoric, sentiment, thought—can become part of another. Even when critics objected to specific interrelations such as the inclusion of epigrams or minor lyrics in the epic,[16] thus limiting the form only to inclusion of features from the noblest poetry (panegyric, divine ode, etc.), they nevertheless accepted interrelations of forms or features of forms.

The source for this view was Aristotle who, in comparing epic to tragedy, pointed out that its plot should "be constructed on dramatic principles." "The parts also, with the exception of song and scenery, are the same." Although Aristotle notes the

[14] "Answer to Davenant's Preface to *Gondibert*," Spingarn, ii, 55, 56.
[15] Trapp, *Lectures on Poetry* (London, 1742 [1713?]), p. 10; also p. 328.
[16] Dryden, ii, 82.

different ends of tragedy and epic, these are defined by the formal possibilities resulting from interrelated parts. Epic is one kind of verse in narrative form; it has no fixed time. Tragedy and epic, Aristotle writes, differ in the sense that "all the elements of an Epic poem are found in Tragedy, but the elements of a Tragedy are not all found in the Epic poem." The principle of comprehensiveness by which tragedy was to be preferred to epic was based on the epic elements being included in tragedy: "superior it is, because it has all the epic elements—it may even use the epic metre—with the music and scenic effects as important accessories. . . ." [17] Thus the principle of interrelation was one of the principles governing tragedy's superiority to epic.

By the mid-seventeenth century, the inherited Renaissance hierarchy of forms had been altered by elevating georgic and satire and lowering the pastoral. For Puttenham the pastoral was an allegorical lyric that sought "under the vaile of homely persons in rude speeches to insinuate and glaunce at greater matters, and such as perchance had not bene safe to have beene disclosed in any other sort. . . ." He referred to the georgic poem only incidentally in a paragraph about "the forme wherein honest and profitable artes and sciences were treated." [18] For Sidney, following Scaliger and Minturno, eclogues or pastorals belonged to genuine poetry. As for the authors of georgic and didactic works, "whether they properly be Poets or no let Grammarians dispute." [19] By the turn of the century the altered hierarchy of forms was frequently endorsed. Addison praised the *Georgics* as "the most complete, elaborate and finished piece of all antiq-

[17] *Poetics*, tr. S. H. Butcher, *Criticism: The Major Texts*, ed. W. J. Bate (New York, 1970), v, p. 22; xiii, p. 34; xxiv, p. 35; xxvi, p. 38.
[18] *The Arte of English Poesie* (1589), Smith, *Elizabethan Critical Essays*, II, 40, 46.
[19] Sidney, I, 159.

uity." [20] Tickell referred to didactic poetry as "this more noble part of Poetry, which is second to Epic alone." [21] Pastoral poetry, on the other hand, had its Virgilian scope reduced and became subject to parody and irony although still defended by some critics. Pope sought to purify the form by disengaging it from the life of man and offering it as an idealization of the past. But his major work dealing with the experience of his time was in the satiric and didactic forms. Trapp sought to explain the changed status of pastoral in the period. He granted the historical scope of pastorals, declaring that its subjects were as various as human passions and that it "may, in some measure, partake of every Kind of Poetry," provided that the scene was in the country and the thoughts not inconsistent with the scene. But he found that in modern times, pastoral was not quite suitable. It was "a Poem less suitable to modern Times, on account of the Difference in the Circumstances of human life, from what it was anciently. As the Condition of Shepherds is now mean and contemptible; it seems too forced a Prosopopoeia to affix to them any Character of Politeness, or to introduce them as Men of Wealth and Education: These Things are contradictory to truth, and therefore leave no Room for Fiction." And with regard to the subject of the didactic poem, he declared, "I would . . . observe that any Thing in the World may be the Subject of this Kind of Poem." [22]

A shift in the importance of georgic forms was part of the

---

[20] "An Essay on Virgil's Georgics" (1697), *The Works of Joseph Addison*, ed. T. Tickell (London, 1804), v, 454.

[21] Thomas Tickell, "De Poesi Didactica," in *Thomas Tickell and the Eighteenth Century Poets (1685–1740)*, by Richard Eustace Tickell (London, 1931), p. 199.

[22] Trapp, pp. 180, 186, 200.

didactic shift,[23] altering the status of satire, epistle, and the fable, as well as that of smaller forms such as the epigram, aphorism, and the maxim, whether in prose or verse. I do not wish to imply that forms have a life of their own, some kind of metaphysical essence. Literary forms are written or spoken by people and they are addressed to people. When poets turn to one form rather than another, when critics defend one kind of hierarchy rather than another, they do so for reasons that are related to personal, public, and professional commitments.

The need for didactic mixtures can be related to the scientific, religious, and political developments of the seventeenth century. The microscope and telescope had enabled man to extend his eye and mind.[24] This extension resulted in a reexamination of external nature in terms of the variety of the seen and the unseen hand of God. Perceptual reconsideration was invoked to explain both the seen and the unseen, the historical present and the historical past. Moreover, the aftermath of the Civil War brought with it a body of controversial literature—in both poetry and prose—as well as appeals to subdue controversy. One solution was for literature to appeal to as many groups as possible, seeking to satisfy each. The premise of social, political, and natural variety had as its basis God's plenitude and the implicit harmony underlying the universe.

[23] R. S. Crane, "Critical and Historical Principles of Literary History," *The Idea of the Humanities* (Chicago, 1967), II, 85. Johnson's *Dictionary* (1765) under "Didascalick," a synonym for "didactic," contains a quotation from Prior indicating the ambiguous interrelation of "didascalick" and "heroick."

[24] See M. H. Nicolson, *Newton Demands the Muse* (Princeton, 1966 [1946]), *Science and Imagination* (Ithaca, N. Y., 1956), and *Breaking of the Circle* (Evanston, Ill., 1950).

The perceptual reconsiderations implicit in such works as *Coopers Hill* and *Upon Appleton House* tied the idea of vision to that of history. Distance, prospect, spectator views—these joined the vocabulary of vision to that of history and society. In fact, the development of a comparative, historical consciousness underlies the didactic shift, the discovered relation between observations of nature and historical retrospection. It is not that Renaissance writers ignored historical change; Bernard Weinberg has shown that sixteenth-century Italian critics were aware of it.[25] But they did not consider change in terms of the scientific, naturalistic as well as political needs of a new audience.

The criterion of propriety or decorum identified literary expression with social action, and social action that distinguished between present and past propriety. Neoclassical critics substituted historical justification for formal ends; the interrelations of forms and the mixtures within forms are defended by comparative procedures, arrived at by distinguishing the propriety of Greek or Latin or Elizabethan usage from neoclassical. Propriety and decorum need to be understood as comparative social and literary terms: the argument, as Pope formulated it, was that what was appropriate for Greek or Roman society or for Shakespeare's audience was not appropriate for his own audience.

The shift to didactic forms can also be understood in terms of the mixtures such forms involve. Varronian satire, for example, was by derivation and by practice a medley, consisting "not only of all kinds of Verse, but of Verse and Prose mix'd together." [26] Its subject matter could include praise and blame, its form panegyric and epigram and maxim, its style could be low and sublime. It is less important that the critics did not

[25] *A History of Literary Criticism in the Italian Renaissance* (Chicago, 1961), II, 1110–11.

[26] Trapp, p. 223. See also Dryden, II, 113.

agree upon the place of satire in the hierarchy than that its place was related to the kind of mixtures it could contain—heroic, burlesque, pastoral. The point to be made here is that these mixtures became, in the works of Augustan writers, related to political and religious factionalism, to a procedure by which different groups could be addressed, with some being supported and others attacked. Such satire in Restoration comedy made use of diverse classes, ideas, and diction and was defended by Farquhar on the grounds that the dramatists must appeal to as many different responders as possible.[27] Types of mixture have also to do with the manner in which past and present meanings are interrelated, the manner in which surface and subsurface can be combined. But more about this later.

The argument from variety also applies to the practice of the periodical essay. And the model of this was, of course, Addison's aim as stated in *Spectator* 10 (12 March 1711): "I shall be ambitious to have it said of me, that I have brought Philosophy out of closets and libraries, schools and colleges, to dwell in clubs and assemblies, at tea-tables, and in coffee-houses." [28] Johnson declared, in *Rambler* Number 23 (5 June 1750), "he who endeavours to gain many readers, must try various arts of invitation, essay every avenue of pleasure, and make frequent changes in his methods of approach." [29] The recognition of a new audience—"many readers"—that had to be won as well as taught

[27] "A Discourse Upon Comedy, in Reference to the English Stage" (1702), *Eighteenth-Century Critical Essays*, ed. Scott Elledge (Ithaca, N. Y.), I, 92–93.

[28] *Works*, I, 32. This passage and the following are quoted in the essay by Roy M. Wiles, "The Periodical Essay: Lures to Readership," *English Symposium Papers*, II (State University of New York at Fredonia, 1972), pp. 3–40.

[29] *The Rambler*, ed. W. J. Bate and Albrecht B. Strauss, *The Works of Samuel Johnson* (New Haven, 1969), III, 129.

accounted for the varied approach of the mixtures in the periodi-
cals. The principle of variation also suggests the need of the
reader to adapt to different works and different situations.
Shaftesbury's reference to a "mixed character," one adaptable to
all things, is to the kind of consciousness that such works can
develop.[30]

J. Paul Hunter has argued that "almost all eighteenth century
literature meant to influence specific attitudes and actions relative to particular events, persons, and ideas, as well as more general loyalties." The popular tradition, for example, included
among its kinds, "guide books, anthologies of examples of God's
judgments and mercies, spiritual autobiographies and biographies, sermons, devotional tracts, meditations upon physical objects, tracts for the times, and treatises arguing almost every
conceivable philosophical, theological or ethical issue." [31]

As an example of the mixture of the smaller poetic didactic
forms with the larger, I point first to the epigram. The fact that
the epigram became part of nondidactic forms was generally accepted. What was not unanimously shared was the approval of
such combinations. John Sheffield, the Duke of Buckingham,
objected to epigram in elegy:

Trifles like these perhaps of late have past,
And may be lik'd awhile, but never last;
'Tis Epigram, 'tis Point, 'tis what you will,
But not an Elegie, nor writ with skill. (110–13) [32]

[30] *The Life, Unpublished Letters and Philosophical Regimen of Anthony, Earl of Shaftesbury*, ed. B. Rand (London, 1900), p. 26.

[31] " 'Peace' and the Augustans: Some Implications of Didactic Method and Literary Form," *Studies in Change and Revolution*, ed. Paul Korshin (London, 1972), pp. 167, 170.

[32] "An Essay Upon Poetry," Spingarn, II, 289.

Addison rejected the propriety of epigram in the ballad. He recognized that the subjects of these poems could be those of the epic or the elegy and he admitted into them features from descriptive poetry, but he drew the line at epigram, remarking that had the "old song been filled with epigrammatical turns and points of wit, it might perhaps have pleased the wrong taste of some readers. . . ." [33] But Addison was clearly cognizant that the epigram, the didactic wit-turn, was infecting nonsatiric forms, for it had already appeared in the lyric, as well as in the epic. Dryden's "Alexander's Feast" and Pope's "Ode for Music on St. Cecilia's Day" did contain epigrammatical turns; later in the century Joseph Warton objected to the fact that these poems conclude with "an epigram of four lines; a species of wit as flagrantly unsuitable to the dignity, and as foreign to the nature, of the lyric, as it is of the epic muse." [34] But some critics, contemporaries of Addison, did consider the epigram as appropriate to the epic; epigrams, wrote Trapp, can "breathe a Spirit of Sublimity, every way becoming them." [35] Didactic features could not only be included in lyrics, but some extended lyrics could be considered as didactic expressions. When Blair listed his four types of ode, one was clearly didactic: "moral and philosophical odes." [36] The didactic element could even be applied to tragedy, not merely in terms of poetic justice, but in the management of the form. Comedy mixed with tragedy, some critics argued, was a clearer approximation to actual life than either of the purer forms. And this is the basis of Johnson's well-known

[33] Addison, *Spectator* 74, *Works*, I, 195.

[34] Warton, *An Essay on the Genius and Writings of Pope* (1756) (London, 1806), I, 60.

[35] Trapp, p. 157.

[36] Hugh Blair, *Lectures on Rhetoric and Belles Lettres* (1783) (London, 1817), III, 131.

defense of the "mingled drama." "That the mingled drama may
convey all the instruction of tragedy or comedy cannot be denied, because it includes both in its alternations of exhibition,
and approaches nearer than either to the appearance of life, by
shewing how great machinations and slender designs may promote or obviate one another, and the high and the low co-
operate in the general system by unavoidable concatenation." [37]

The neoclassical interrelation of poems and parts within
poems resulted in the redefining of older forms. Traditional pastorals came to be seen as combinations of forms. With regard to
Theocritus' *Idylls* and Virgil's *Eclogues*, for example, the procedure was to subdivide these works into discrete poems, thus permitting a new definition of pastoral that would not clash with
tradition. Eighteenth-century critics pointed out that the "idyl-
lium," the kind of poem Theocritus wrote, meant not "pastoral"
but little scenes or pictures, applicable to many kinds of subjects
in nature. And the name that Virgil used for his early poems,
Eclogae, was by derivation a term for "select poems," and if
they were to be restricted to poems about shepherds, they need
not be confined to a specific subject matter like the "Golden
Age." The argument for and against pastorals—the publication
of ironic "pastorals" such as *The Beggar's Opera*, or attempts to
modernize the form—illustrate the introduction of a didactic
(here satiric) version of what had been a lyric poem. Even when
Pope sought to present himself as a conservator of pastoral conventions, he found it necessary to "use some illusion to render a
Pastoral delightful; and this consists in exposing the best side
only of a shepherd's life, and in concealing its miseries." [38] The

[37] Johnson, "Preface" (1765) to Shakespeare, *Works*, VII, 67.
[38] "A Discourse on Pastoral Poetry" (1709), *The Poems of Alexander
Pope*, ed. John Butt (New Haven, 1963), p. 120.

rationale of the ideal was didactic, applied to his audience and to his time.

By mid-century, the combination or mixtures of forms and parts of forms had come to be taken for granted. When Bishop Lowth came to discuss the sacred poetry of the Bible, it was apparent that this was a model of mixed religious forms. Even within the psalms themselves, Bishop Lowth discovered many kinds. The Book of Psalms, he wrote, "is a collection, under the general title of hymns to the praise of God, containing poems of different kinds, and elegies among the rest." [39]

Bringing the old forms into a new hierarchy and providing explanations for the new forms that resulted, the critics and authors argued for the "newness," the "new sort of writing" of the poetry and prose. Thus Thomas Sprat wrote of Cowley's pindaric odes that they "may perhaps be thought rather a new sort of Writing," [40] the newness being the swiftness of transition, the sudden shifts of level. In his "Apology" to *A Tale of a Tub,* Swift wrote (and the irony supports my contention of repeated claims to newness) that he "resolved to proceed in a manner, that should be altogether new, the World having been already too long nauseated with endless Repetitions upon every Subject." [41] This newness included the mixing of prose fiction with nonfictional narrative, the parody of varied forms, the mixing of allegory with scatology. Fielding, in the preface to *Joseph Andrews,* declared, "it may not be improper to premise a few words

[39] Robert Lowth, *Lectures on the Sacred Poetry of the Hebrews,* tr. by G. Gregory (London, 1787), II, 144.

[40] "Account of the Life and Writings of Abraham Cowley" (1668), Spingarn, II, 132.

[41] *A Tale of a Tub,* ed. A. C. Guthkelch and D. Nichol Smith (Oxford, 1920), p. 4.

concerning this kind of writing, which I do not remember to have seen hitherto attempted in our language." [42] And Johnson in the life of Denham declared that Denham was the author of a new species of composition "of which the fundamental subject is some particular landscape to be poetically described, with the addition of such embellishments as may be supplied by historical retrospection or incidental meditation." [43] I need not point out that "historical retrospection" could include panegyric, elegy, and didactic exposition, and that "incidental meditation" could be expressed in hymns and psalms.

A new combination can be understood as a demonstration of authorial individuality. The particular combination that Johnson described had political implications because it treated landed estates as prospects from which to view past and present. The estate could be a perceptual viewpoint as well as a mediating position between past and future. Thus the particular variety it encompassed tended to support the role of the gentry.

II. THE INDIVIDUALITY OF FORMS

I have been arguing that within the hierarchy of kinds, the major forms often included the minor. I now wish to argue that major and minor forms were interrelated in terms of their parts or features: all or some could embrace, in addition to common subject matter and characters noted above, portions of a shared diction, a shared rhetoric, a shared procedure for allusions, and a shared style. In fact, the distinction between "form" and

[42] *Joseph Andrews and Shamela*, ed. Martin C. Battestin (Boston, 1961), p. 7.
[43] *Lives of the Poets*, ed. G. Birkbeck Hill (Oxford, 1905), I, 77.

"mode" can make this clear. "Form" refers to a combination of means to lead to a specific effect; "mode" refers to kinds of means. Thus there is a pastoral form—Pope's or Phillips' "Pastorals"—but pastoral as a mode can apply to different poetic kinds—to "Lycidas," a pastoral elegy, to drama, *As You Like It*, to prose fiction, *Arcadia*, to selected features of the pastoral form such as descriptions of shepherds or nature. And the pastoral form itself could include panegyric and elegiac elements and satiric subject matter; it did not exclude even the epigram. Rosalie Colie remarked of Renaissance poetry that there was an art to be mastered for the eclogue form and the pastoral mode, for tragedy as a form and the tragic mode. "Those arts mastered," she wrote, "there is no reason other than conviction why they should not be used together—but they cannot be used with utter indiscriminateness. We have to know *why* they are intermixed." [44] The distinction of form and mode that applied to pastoral applied equally to satire and the georgic poem. The form-mode distinction can be understood as an interpretative procedure. The mode of pastoral or satire presupposed a knowledge of the whole form, and in that way a satiric passage depended upon a depth knowledge of the form in order to explain the mode. For example, it gave the mode of satire an interrelation with all synchronic forms that could include it as well as with satire as a form. The form-mode distinction, therefore, functioned synchronically in contrast, for example, with a feature like allusion to a past work, which functioned diachronically. The interrelation of forms, therefore, provides a basis for interpretation that distinguishes the language of surface struc-

[44] Colie, *The Resources of Kind*, p. 116. See also Paul Alpers' mistaken attempt to regularize the use of "mode" in "Mode in Narrative Poetry," *To Tell a Story: Narrative Theory and Practice*, William Andrews Clark Memorial Library (Los Angeles, 1973), pp. 25–56.

ture from that which draws attention to itself as part of a past work or other contemporary genre. Thus translations, reworkings of Latin passages, become part both of the continuity of literature in this period and the basis for recognizing different levels in the linguistic code. Moreover, the form-mode distinction, especially in satire, georgic, and mixed prose forms, introduces referential truth into literature to combine with nonreferential.

The point is that interrelations among forms were reenforced by the form-mode distinction since modes of satire, for example, could appear in most other forms. The specification of parts of any form was minimally defined, and it was precisely because this specification of parts was left open that the critics relied upon "propriety" and "decorum" as comparative (historical) guides. These concepts need to be understood as hypothetical constructs dependent upon the critic's specific application. The effectiveness of any assemblage of parts was determined by the critic's adherence to a view of unity that specified interrelations. Whether one welcomed or opposed greater freedom of transition in some forms rather than others, resisted or welcomed the diction of one form in another, the grounds of the criticism led back to the justification of God's and man's variety.

Since genres or forms were interrelated, it is self-evident that each genre had a specific identity. How was this identity determined? Bernard Weinberg concludes his discussion of sixteenth-century Italian practical criticism by drawing attention to the community of problems treated:

> Among such problems, the most important was that of the genres; it took several forms. For each of the Italian works, the disputants had to decide to what genre it belonged. If it was an old, recognized genre, then one must ask whether the work satisfactorily fulfilled the traditional requirements of the

genre. If it was a new genre, then it was appropriate to inquire whether it should be admitted to the canon of legitimate and proper genres, how it should be practised, on the basis of what analogies to the old genres its conditions should be circumscribed. Sometimes it was extremely difficult to assign the work to any genre, and lengthy descriptions of the work and definitions of the genre had to precede a solution. At all times the solution involved those same topics that were foremost in theoretical discussion: the nature of poetry and its ends, criteria, and precepts for practice. Frequently, several quarrels came to turn about the same genre, thus creating an immediate community of problems.[45]

The problem of genre involved at least two distinctions: one was to identify the class of works that belonged to poetry and the other was to identify specific kinds within this class. The first, therefore, inevitably made interrelations possible among all poems; the second drew attention to the number of specific interrelations between different genres. Every new genre involved a synchronic relation to the other genres, and each traditional genre had a diachronic history as well as a synchronic one.

Eighteenth-century critics, like Trapp, saw the forms as hierarchical, comprehensively embodied or capable of being harmoniously embodied in the drama or epic. One theory of forms, therefore, identified the kinds by their appropriate means and ends in the harmony. Another theory of harmony that critics carried into the eighteenth century was that of a concord resulting from apparent discord (*concordia discors*). It, too, necessarily embodied a mixture of divergent features, and it was used didactically to support the combination of oppositions. Critics like Blair, who argued for the specificity of forms, recognized that even within the ode, somewhat different effects could be

[45] Weinberg, II, 1108.

achieved by altering means, for example, the subject matter. In order for an identity to be specified, it had to be seen as related to other forms and as distinct from them. The eighteenth-century intermixtures extended far beyond those specified in the Renaissance; and not only were they more didactic, they also included new types of such mixtures. Among these were new forms such as the periodical essay, the novel, prose fictions, and the altered older forms such as the georgic and the epistle.

This concept of kinds or genre granted that the kinds had specific effects, but these tended to become loosened in terms of the interrelations possible for each kind. Inevitably the extension of the parts that could fit a form led to the alteration of the effect of that form. There are four types of interrelation that I wish to illustrate: diction, rhetoric, allusion, and style. One of the commonest aspects of interrelations among eighteenth-century poetry was the use of different dictions within a "kind." In this respect, Pope's remark to Spence about the purity of diction in his pastorals merits quotation: "Though Virgil, in his pastorals, has sometimes six or eight lines together that are epic: I have been so scrupulous as scarce ever to admit above two together, even in the Messiah." Upon this Geoffrey Tillotson has remarked: "Mixing the kinds, he [Pope] knew what he was doing and marked off the component parts by the use of different kinds of diction (diction brings with it other linguistic modes such as personification, apostrophe, exclamation)." [46] This view of limited interchangeability of diction was not only taken for granted by the critics of the eighteenth century, it was practiced by the writers.

As an example of the manner in which diction from pastoral and elegy was applied to diverse forms, I quote a recurrent

[46] *Augustan Poetic Diction* (London, 1964), p. 25.

image in seventeenth- and eighteenth-century poetry, first noted in 1785 by John Scott of Amwell,[47] and recently by James Sutherland who uses the image as an example of the "way in which an eighteenth-century poet willingly availed himself of 'happy combinations of words' and 'phrases poetically elegant in the English language.' " [48] The image is of flowers that bloom, unseen, in the desert.

If the hypothesis that each kind had its own diction were true, it would be unlikely that a figure such as the desert flower would be found in a love song by Waller, a mock-heroic epic by Pope, a fable by Ambrose Philips, a satire by Young, a georgic by Thomson, an elegy by Gray, and a didactic poem by Dyer.

Waller's song "Go, lovely Rose" (1645) is an address to the rose that is an ironic song of love:

Tell her that's young,
And shuns to have her Graces spy'd,
    That hadst thou sprung
In Desarts where no men abide,
    Thou must have uncommended dy'd. (6–10)

Pope's "rose" occurs in a passage spoken by Belinda under the influence of "beauteous grief" at the loss of her lock:

Oh had I rather un-admir'd remain'd
In some lone Isle, or distant *Northern* Land;
Where the gilt *Chariot* never marks the Way,
Where none learn *Ombre*, none e'er taste *Bohea*!
There kept my Charms conceal'd from mortal Eye,
Like Roses that in Desarts bloom and die. (IV, 153–58)

[47] *Critical Essays on Some of the Poems of Several English Poets* (London, 1785), p. 206.
[48] Sutherland, *A Preface to Eighteenth Century Poetry*, pp. 132–33.

Ambrose Philips in "The Fable of Thule" wrote:

> Half human thus by lineage, half divine,
> In forests did the lovely beauty shine,
> Like woodland flowers which paint the desert glades
> And waste their sweets in unfrequented shades. (37–40)

Ten years later (1728), in a satire on women in the *Universal Passion*, Young wrote:

> How gay *they* smile! Such blessings *nature* pours,
> O'erstock'd mankind enjoy but half her stores:
> In distant wilds, by human eyes unseen,
> She rears her flow'rs, and spreads her velvet green:
> Pure gurgling rills the lonely desert trace,
> And *waste* their music on the savage race. (v, 163–68)

In the *Autumn* pastoral narrative about Lavinia, Thomson wrote in the revised 1744 version:

> As in the hollow Breast of Appenine
> Beneath the Shelter of encircling Hills,
> A Myrtle rises, far from human Eye,
> And breathes its balmy Fragrance o'er the Wild;
> So flourished blooming, and unseen by all,
> The sweet Lavinia. (210–15)

Gray's "Elegy" (1750) contains the most famous of the unseen flower lines:

> Full many a gem of purest ray serene
> The dark unfathomed caves of ocean bear:
> Full many a flower is born to blush unseen
> And waste its sweetness on the desert air. (53–56)

And John Dyer in *The Fleece* (1757), a didactic poem, in a passage dealing with the journey through Russia, wrote:

> and on each hand
> Roads hung with carcases, or under foot
> Thick strown; while, in their rough bewildered vales,
> The blooming rose its fragrance breathes in vain,
> And silver fountains fall, and nightingales
> Attune their notes, where none are left to hear. (IV, 418–23)

The flower born to blush unseen is a topos that is not, so far as its diction is concerned, species bound. The image stands for the possibilities of nature that can either be used or misused. It forms a part of the large body of eighteenth-century retirement imagery that sees innocence as a consequence of one's natural situation rather than as deliberate rejection of unpleasant situations or the sacrifice of one possibility in order to retain others. The image is an example of God's fruitfulness at the same time that it suggests the unavailability of this variety to men; such an example, therefore, suggests that God's "Nature is but Art, unknown to thee." [49] The diction that derives from a language about nature in the pastoral can fit the song, elegy, satire, georgic, fable, pastoral, and mock-heroic; its maneuverability rests on the potentiality of forms to accommodate perceptual responses to nature as a norm. Each form had some kinds of diction considered appropriate to it, but the interrelation of the diction explains how the forms could be understood as resembling, comprehending, enhancing, or even contrasting with one another.

When Wordsworth continued the flower image in "Lucy Gray," it was concealed in a metaphor:

[49] *Essay on Man*, Epistle I, l. 289.

No Mate, no comrade Lucy knew;
She dwelt on a wild Moor,
The sweetest thing that ever grew
Beside a human door!

The metaphor places Lucy within nature, a procedure that differed from the didactic separation of man from nature, a separation identified by the interaction of one kind of nature (flowers)
with another ("distant wilds" or "desert air"). The response of
the speaker to Lucy is to hold out the ambiguous possibility of
her continued presence, like a natural force. This ambiguity,
this mysterious possibility, is not, of course, the same limitation
to be found in the unavailable beauty of eighteenth-century imagery.

The shift in implication can, perhaps, be used to indicate how
even a pastoral image in the eighteenth century is used "didactically"—that is, to underline the apparent "waste" of nature, to
draw attention to the need for belief and acceptance. For Wordsworth, the image becomes an instance of the extraordinary possibilities of the ordinary. The "footmarks" are the signs not of
nature's limits, but of the manner in which nature's death-marks
(her limitations) may become life-marks. Geoffrey H. Hartman
refers to the Lucy poems by saying that "Lucy's fulfillment by
nature and her passing into it (her death) coincide." [50] And he
draws attention to the role of the speaker whose consciousness is
altered by Lucy's death. The eighteenth-century speaker must
again and again acknowledge and accept the limitation of
"waste" and "death." What is apparent, then, is the manner in
which the topos functions when it is part of the eighteenth-century hierarchy dominated by didactic forms and when it becomes part of the hierarchy dominated by lyrical forms.

[50] *Wordsworth's Poetry 1787–1814* (New Haven, 1964), p. 158.

The examples I have been giving of mixtures within forms apply to prose as well as poetry. The features of subject or language could fit more than one end. Thus the language of burlesque and parody, according to Fielding, could be admitted into his comic epic in prose on the grounds of the diverse audiences (here the classical reader is invoked). In his preface to *Joseph Andrews* he wrote: "In the diction, I think, burlesque itself may be sometimes admitted" in order to titillate "the classical reader, for whose entertainment those parodies or burlesque imitations are chiefly calculated." But he declared that "we have carefully excluded it from our sentiments and characters; for there it is never properly introduced, unless in writings of the burlesque kind." [51] The point that Fielding makes is that the mixed diction is directed at the classical audience, but that burlesque mixtures are not able to be tolerated in the characters or sentiments of a comic epic. Other mixtures, such as the use of inset stories and the introductory essays, were, however, acceptable practices, too common to be noted in the preface.

I wish to draw attention here to the principle of interrelation as it can appear in fiction. The levels of diction that Fielding permits are only one aspect of the variety of interrelation his novels reveal. For interrelation of characters—the relation between Parson Adams and Parson Trulliber in *Joseph Andrews*, or the relation among the varied innkeepers in *Tom Jones*—is based on the principle of degrees of difference within similarity. Interrelation that is necessary to distinction can be considered a principle of knowledge, a method of distinguishing by degrees of comparison. Characters, like diction, can reveal subtle differences by the interrelation of levels.

Discussions of diction should be distinguished from rhetorical

[51] Fielding, p. 8.

features that could be applied to any form, though both are
types of interrelation. Bishop Lowth, for example, pointed out
that antithetic parallelism—"when a thing is illustrated by its
contrary being opposed to it"—is "not confined to any particular
form; for sentiments are opposed to sentiments, words to words,
singulars to singulars, plurals to plurals. . . ." [52] This feature
of style can occur in proverbs as it can in the superior kinds of
Hebrew poetry. And although it is not frequent in sublime poetry, Bishop Lowth quotes several examples from Isaiah:

> In a little anger have I forsaken thee;
> But with great mercies will I receive thee again.
> In a short wrath I hid my face for a moment from thee
> But with everlasting kindness will I have mercy on thee.[53]

Rhetorical features that can appear in all forms provide yet
another basis for harmony. If "antithetical parallelism" could
apply to all forms, though to some more readily than to others,
so, too, could repetition, allusion, and other figures. Bishop
Lowth refers to rhetorical figures, but even specific images like
that of the desert flower could appear in most kinds. The extension of a rhetorical feature or a specific diction was governed by
propriety of function. The relation of part to whole, the manner
in which a part could be fitted into the poem in terms of transition, combination, and effect, formed the basis for its approval
or disapproval.

This is the point at which to introduce the concept of the
sublime style as a feature locatable in the various kinds. Of the
five sources or springheads of the sublime listed by Longinus,
three are the result of art. The last of these related to connection

---

[52] Lowth, ii, 45.   [53] Lowth, ii, 48.

of selected parts to produce sublimity in the whole composition: "Now, as there are no Subjects, which are not attended by some adherent Circumstances, an accurate and judicious Choice of the most suitable of these Circumstances, and an ingenious and skil- ful Connexion of them into one Body, must necessarily produce the Sublime. For what by the judicious Choice, and what by the skilful Connexion, they cannot but very much affect the Imagi- nation." [54]

The translator, William Smith, makes clear that he interprets "judicious choice" as applicable to a poem as a whole as well as to narrative divisions. Thus he refers to Adam and Eve in *Para- dise Lost* as the "finest Picture of conjugal Love." "In its Serenity and Sun-shine, it is noble, amiable, endearing and innocent." [55] Such a passage could be found in drama as well as epic, in heroic epistle as well as in odes or pastorals. The other two sources of art were figures and noble expression (choice of words and diction).

These formed sublime passages in their effect upon the reader or hearer, and one such example can be found in the allusion to a moment of immobility—a marble moment—in *Eloisa to Abe- lard*. Eloisa's cry: "I have not yet forgot my self to stone" (1. 24) is an allusion to *Il Penseroso:* "Forget thyself to marble" (1. 42), a line in which the goddess of melancholy is described in her accustomed state:

Thy rapt soul sitting in thine eyes:
There held in holy passion still,
Forget thyself to marble.

[54] *Dionysius Longinus on the Sublime*, tr. William Smith (London, 1743), p. 27.
[55] Ibid., p. 136.

The propriety of the allusion rests on the kind of poem Pope is writing: the Ovidian epistle, a type of poem that because of its emotive contrasts could incorporate sublime expressions. "It is, indeed, no other," declares Joseph Warton, "than a passionate soliloquy, in which the mind gives vent to the distresses and emotions under which it labours. . . . Judgment is chiefly shewn, by opening the interesting complaint just at such a period of time, as will give occasion for the most tender sentiments, and the most sudden and violent turns of passion, to be displayed." [56] The line from the pastoral suits the situation of passion while at the same time providing Pope with ironic overtones since Eloisa is a nun without the purity or the calmness of serene Melancholy, and the "stone" is not "marble."

The propriety of allusions depends on the comprehensive range of diction in the epistle. The allusion moves beyond the single line to the two poetic kinds—the pastoral and the heroic epistle—as spoken addresses (dramatic monologues). One is addressed to contemplation and the consistent values of meditative melancholy. The other is addressed to the speaker's self with her inconsistent turns of meditation and melodrama. The common feature is the expression of meditation, and it is the different ends of pastoral and epistle that make Pope's irony possible. This point can be supported by reference to the mock epic and its requirement of a knowledge of the epic in order that the parody or irony be understood.

Augustan writers use allusion not merely to draw attention to species relations (parody and mock heroic) but to indicate competitive adaptation of a classical phrase or passage to the present situation. In this respect allusion resembles the concept of accretion of knowledge by degree because it is the degree of alteration or distortion that gives the allusion its significance. In addition,

[56] Warton, I, 282–83.

allusion is a form of "historical retrospection" because it calls attention to a past that is usable in the poet's present situation. And thus the concept of interrelation and intermixture is applied to historical as well as formal understanding.

Allusion, as it presents itself for interpretation, belongs to a different coding procedure from common rhetorical devices and themes. It belongs to the past used in the present to distinguish it from the present—as in translated passages from Virgil or Horace or Juvenal. It thus is part of the subsurface structure of historical meaning the form possesses, providing a guide to the comparative basis of the two poems (and societies) since two types of propriety or decorum are being intermingled.

If we accept the principle that a line from a pastoral poem can be appropriate to an epistle, and if the line retains some of its original context, then the notion of unity implied cannot be "indivisible." It is a unity that permits associations that are appropriate, and thus each work is a combination of features governed by the criteria of fitness to the passage and the form. This can only be judged in terms of how transitions are made, and this is, indeed, one of the considerations of this criticism. In Warton's discussion of an *Essay on Criticism*, he declared that each of the precepts "naturally introduce the succeeding ones, so as to form an entire whole." And he invoked Richard Hurd on Horace's *Epistle to the Pisos* in which "the connexions are delicately fine, and almost imperceptible, like the secret hinges of a well-wrought box, yet they artfully and closely unite each part together, and give coherence, uniformity and beauty to the work." [57] And Johnson in his *Dictionary* characterized the "greater ode" by "sublimity, rapture and quickness of transition." [58]

[57] Warton, I, 97–98.
[58] Quoted by Maclean, "From Action to Image," p. 419.

The principles of unity, therefore, whether of the didactic poem or ode, were governed by types of connection or association. These could be contrast, or resemblance, or cause and effect, or place and consequence, or time and its relations; indeed, as the century proceeded, the types of possible connection or transition grew so extensive that at the end of the century Dugald Stewart recognized that any relations could be associated provided the proper transitions were made. The hierarchy of forms thus became ambiguous, and many of the individual distinctions among elegy, ode, panegyric, song, idyll, georgic, satire were eroded so that when Wordsworth set up his six groups in 1815, one, narrative, was a new class; the dramatic included opera and the lyric excluded pastoral; and the last three, the Idyllic, the Didactic, and Philosophic Satire, could be recognized as the basis for a new "composite order" of poems "of which Young's *Night Thoughts* and Cowper's *Task*, are excellent examples." [59]

The shift from a hierarchy adapted to didactic forms to one adjusted to lyric forms can be best noted in the ascendancy of the lyric and the decline of epic and dramatic forms. The lyric becomes, in the early nineteenth century, dominated by the principle of pure or spontaneous poetry. The didactic forms are, then, self-evident composites of purity and impurity. The associative or combinatory unity of the didactic poem is seen as a collection of fragments in contrast to the organic unfolding of the lyric.

As a result of the variety within works due to the subjects and to the mixtures, the transitions and combinations led to procedures for emphatic closures. Some works could be associatively

---

[59] "Preface to Poems (1815)," *Wordsworth's Literary Criticism*, ed. Nowell C. Smith (London, 1925 [1905]), p. 153.

expanded; the author sought for an assertive conclusion, one that clearly announced and satisfied the need for a conclusion, if, indeed, anything was to be concluded. The announcement of the "conclusion" to *A Tale of a Tub* or the insistent conclusion of *The Dunciad* deomonstrates this procedure.

Barbara H. Smith, in dealing with the closural force of unqualified assertions, writes that "when universals and absolutes (words such as 'all,' 'none,' 'only,' and 'always') occur in assertions, they are themselves the expressions of the speaker's inability or refusal to qualify. . . . All such nonqualifying words and phrases tend to have closural effects when they occur as terminal features in an utterance or a poem, for they not only reinforce our sense of the speaker's conviction but are themselves expressions of comprehensiveness, climax, or finality." [60] She quotes the conclusion of the 1742 *Dunciad* as an example of such closure. I believe this argument is sound, but it needs amplification in dealing with Augustan poems. Closure needs to be asserted because, within the poem, additions can be and are fully and frequently made. *The Rape of the Lock, The Seasons, The Pleasures of the Imagination* were like *The Dunciad* expanded poems with strong closures, but the closure did not prevent expansion of the varied means. Interrelations and intermixtures could be increased and one of the consequences was that the conclusion had to be asserted in an unqualified way. Within the body of *The Dunciad* revisions could be and were made. The *Dunciad Variorum* of 1729 concluded:

"In vain! they gaze, turn giddy, rave, and die.
Thy hand great Dulness! lets the curtain fall,
And universal Darkness covers all."

[60] *Poetic Closure* (Chicago, 1968), p. 183.

> "Enough! enough!" the raptur'd Monarch cries;
> And thro' the Ivory Gate the Vision flies.

Although Pope added a fourth book to *The Dunciad* in 1742, the ending remained equally assertive:

> Thy hand, great Anarch! lets the curtain fall;
> And Universal Darkness buries All.

The kind of unity that "Species" criticism propounded can be understood from Pope's didactic *Essay on Criticism*. The passage on the "Whole" reads as follows:

> A perfect Judge will *read* each work of Wit
> With the same spirit that its Author writ,
> Survey the Whole, nor seek slight Faults to find,
> Where *Nature moves*, and *Rapture warms*, the Mind. (233–36)

The ends of the poem are to explain what proper criticism is and who the model practitioners were and are. These two couplets form part of an explanation of the faults, for "Whoever thinks a faultless Piece to see, / Thinks what ne'er was, nor is, nor e'er shall be" (ll. 253–54). The different species imitate different kinds of human action, and the underlying metaphor of this imitation, for Pope, is a poem as a body with an informing soul or spirit that is "*it self unseen*, but in the Effects, remains" (l. 79). The moving quality of poetry, its vigor, resides in the manner in which parts combine, join, or unite. Parts should neither be regularly dull nor monstrously irregular, but between regularity and monstrosity there looms the theory of species. Nature to all things "fix'd the Limits fit" (l. 52), but the "fixity"—the rules— were governed by interrelations and the discovery of the limits depended upon the knowledge of acceptable interrelations. Of course, each species was distinct in the sense that it had its own end (however ambiguous this was). But many of the features were interrelated with other forms so that "distinctness" was a matter of degree rather than of kind. And all forms were part of a family of forms, rather than distinct or isolated species. Critics who ignore this interrelationship whether by thinking of species as pure or denying that the concept of species is useful for us are both wrong. Species were part of an interrelated hierarchy and the parts of each species were related to others. Species were not "pure" even though critics sought to make them "pure" by reducing mixtures. But a theory of kinds is necessary if we are to understand how, and in what ways, eighteenth-century works can be interpreted.

Pope warned against making the whole "depend upon a Part," but he was aware of the need to make the parts unite; and this meant that the parts themselves—the figures, the meter, the light and dark shading—had to be carefully worked. The features that helped give life to forms—the careful sublime, the proper turn of wit, the description of detail and of the prospect, and, indeed, all the figures of poetry—became a source for inquiry because their various usages demanded distinctions between minute eccentricity and acceptable individuality within the range of the species. As time went on, these discriminations became more refined. And the increased refinement made the distinction of effect difficult to sustain.

III. THE MODEL APPLIED

In the late seventeenth and eighteenth centuries, "kind" was identified by its effect upon the reader, but since the higher forms could include the lower, "kinds" clearly could have multiple effects. The lower forms were interrelated in terms of their parts—character, subject matter, diction, and style—and thus the forms could be seen as sharing qualities, styles, and intermediate as against final effects. This concept of form meant that any particular kind was a combination of features, only the minimum of which was identified with the "kind" itself, and even this minimum was not agreed upon by all critics. Each form could, therefore, be understood as a combination or association joined together for a given effect. But whether that effect was achieved depended on the kinds of transitions, the idea of propriety or decorum that the critic held. No critic denied mixtures or interrelations, but some claimed that the "purity" of form was to be obtained by limiting the mixtures from other forms.

In this section I shall discuss how eighteenth-century critics saw the historical development of interrelations of forms, and how two new forms support the premise I have been arguing.

The ascendancy of mixed didactic forms in the Augustan period can, perhaps, be understood in terms of the more general theory of the progress of literature. According to Hugh Blair, for example, odes, hymns, elegies, panegyrics, epics, and tragedies were originally all one.

> None of these kinds of poetry, however, were in the first ages of society properly distinguished or separated, as they are now, from each other. Indeed, not only were the different kinds of poetry then mixed together, but all that we now call letters, or composition of any kind, was then blended in one mass. . . . When the progress of society brought on a separation of the different arts and professions of civil life, it led also by degrees to a separation of the different literary provinces from each other.[61]

[61] Blair, *Lectures on Rhetoric and Belles Lettres*, III, 91–92.

Blair was not the only critic who identified all the forms as originally one, gradually assuming individual identities as society became organized into arts and professions. Poetic forms, argued these critics, had their genesis in social forms so that subsequently successful interrelations became instances of civilized harmony whereas their unfortunate mixtures—for example, Addison's remarks on the epigram included in "Chevy Chase"—were forms of disharmony. The progress was, then, from homogeneity to heterogeneity; when the principle is reversed one gets a work like *A Tale of a Tub* which begins with clearly distinguished narrative and digressive sections that become indistinguishable. It moves from heterogeneity to homogeneity.

The interrelation of forms has not often been noted, and Ronald Paulson, one of the few who do note this, connects the seventeenth-century anatomy, sermon, polemical pamphlet, and heroic drama. But he does so to argue that in "all of these forms detail takes on a greater autonomy than is always consistent with the over-all aim of the work." [62] Paulson is correct in identifying features of mixed forms, but inaccurate in assuming that mixtures are forms of disorder.

Among the mixed forms not often noticed are the annotated editions of Greek, Latin, and English authors. Although these were inherited from the Renaissance, in the seventeenth and eighteenth centuries they were frequently addressed to audiences for purposes of edification. Indeed, at the end of the century (1795), Vicesimus Knox argued for the validity of "miscellanies" through the sanction of past works such as Seneca's *Epistles* and Horace's *Sermones*. "Nor let the grave and austere despise them as trifling amusements only . . ." he wrote. "For

[62] *Theme and Structure in Swift's Tale of a Tub* (New Haven, 1960), p. 25.

the mind is nourished by variety of food . . . like the body by a commixture of fish, flesh, fowl, and vegetables." [63]

Both the annotations and miscellanies were parodied in works such as *A Tale of a Tub*, *Tom Thumb*, and *The Dunciad*. And the parody of *A Tale of a Tub*, for example, was to undermine false mixtures (of learning and religion) and, by implication, to suggest proper ones.

The first edition of *A Tale* was published in 1704; the fifth, with "An Apology" and additional notes, was issued in 1710. The latter work is the result of multiple authorship, or so we are led to believe: the Grub Street author, the bookseller, the group of commentators, and, in the 1710 Apology, the author behind the Grub Street author. The forms include, in addition to the Apology, a dedication by the "Bookseller," an address of the "Bookseller to the Reader," a dedicatory epistle to Prince Posterity by the author, a "Preface," and a narrative in the form of a folk tale that turns into an allegory, a series of digressive essays, and a body of annotations. Of course, the prefaces are parodies of Dryden's procedures, but they function as do the digressions, to create disjunctions in the reading of the narrative which begins as a folk tale: "Once upon a Time, there was a Man who had Three Sons by one Wife, and all at a Birth. . . ." But it is a tale never finished: "I can only assure thee, Courteous Reader, for both our Comforts, that my Concern is altogether equal to thine, for my Unhappiness in losing, or mislaying among my Papers the remaining Part of these Memoirs. . . ." [64]

Not only is the narrative of the brothers unfinished, but the irresponsibility revealed in the failure to keep the memoir together is unreproved. The narrative is based on papers—a

[63] "On some Peculiarities in Periodical Essays," *Winter Evenings* (1788), 3rd ed. (London, 1795), 1, 27.

[64] Swift, p. 204.

memoir—by an unreliable keeper, who lacks respect for the past, yet who sees as his task the justification and restoration of the "Grub Street Brotherhood."

The *Tale* with its many forms is, on one level, an attempt to provide a justification of Grub Street writing by a cooperative authorship, with Wotton and others explaining the difficult passages of the tale and digressions. But on another level, the serial reading of the *Tale* is interrupted for the reader, the different forms are monstrous and they interfere with an understanding of the allegory, and, finally, in Section xi, they become mingled and destroy the harmony of form.

The disharmony of forms has its source in the failure of the Grub Street writer to discriminate true from false values of the past, just as the brothers are involved in the over-refined interpretation of the father's will and their consequent disregard of it. Both their disregard and, on the part of two brothers, their restoration of the will come from the pressures of their situations, not from a respect for or admiration of the father.

The interrelation of narrative and digression arises from an attempt to justify a "Brotherhood" that has become divided in itself, and the diversity of forms is an attempt to restore the eminence of one faction. But the consequence of this indiscriminate diversity is to alienate the reader and to create in him an opposition to this type of false learning. Swift indicates the manner in which diversity becomes madness, in which dismembered fragments form a grotesque harmony, whether it is the confluence of garbage in "A Description of a City Shower" or the confluence of narrative and digression in *A Tale*.

In *A Tale* the narrative itself becomes a form of digression, the object being to indicate the historical discontinuity, the corruption of judgment and, finally, the corruption of human responsibility. I believe John Clark is right when he says that in "Section xi all coherence is gone. In a climax of sorts, tale and digression merge, become confounded." [65] The idea of a "digression" or a "wandering" belongs with the mingling of forms to suggest a harmony or a disharmony. The associated terms were "incident," "episode," and "diversion," the first referring to events in which the characters advance the main action of an epic, the second referring to actions collateral to the main one; "diversion," another of the metaphors of wandering, indicates that the author has turned from the narrative to relieve the tension of the reader or to provide him with a new object of interest. The diversion can be another narrative or an essay or, as is claimed in the "Preface" to A Tale, it can refer to the whole work: "at a Grand Committee, some Days ago, this important Discovery was made by a certain curious and refined Observer; That Seamen have a Custom when they meet a *Whale*, to fling him out an empty *Tub*, by way of Amusement, to divert him from laying violent Hands upon the Ship." [66]

The digression essay as a form belongs not only to the mingling of species in this period, but to Swift's special way of thinking about such mixtures. He seems obsessed with the transformations of norms to abnorms, of diversions to deviations. If we consider the use of forms in *Gulliver's Travels*, we can recognize that the four voyages are all forms that digress; they detail Gulliver's wanderings from the destinations for which he sets sail, but, contrariwise, he always returns to England from which he sets out. The repetitive digressions, each a narrative of interest in its own right, ultimately lead to alienation at home. I do not mean to imply that the voyages result in increasing alienation or that *Gulliver's Travels* is organized by any

[65] John R. Clark, *Form and Frenzy in Swift's Tale of a Tub* (Ithaca, (N. Y., 1970), p. 140.
[66] Swift, p. 40.

plan of progression. Rather, the voyaging or wandering accidentally leads Gulliver to a country that he admires. Being prepared there to desist from wandering, he is compelled once again to set forth. It is this sense of frustrated desire that makes his return a digressive voyage. What was previously a return to recognition becomes now a return to alienation.

The multiple authorship of *A Tale of a Tub* leads Denis Donoghue to suggest that the author is really anonymous. But this is to misunderstand the place of multiple authorship, whether fictitious as here, or actual as in the Scriblerus papers or the numerous poetical miscellanies. This authorship is used by Swift to insist on quite different identities that become entangled and unfortunately fused. Authors can be seen in prefaces, for example, that introduce poets, as quite properly maintaining their identity, decorum, and honesty. But not in *A Tale*, where the authors of the notes, the bookseller, the digressor are part of a family of falsely learned men and corrupted critics who perpetrate such works on readers.

The brotherhood is indeed the corrupted family of which the three brothers represent the model—one birth leading to three sons and many scholars leading to one misshapen birth. In its concern with sects and factions, *A Tale* is not only about the kinds of learned folly in a commonwealth, it is a fable of civil war, with brother plotting against brother.

Swift's use of forms is representative of the factionalism of society, and the dangers of this division. Addison, while agreeing on the existence of factions, sought to mediate among them in his writings. Indeed, this is precisely the use of forms developed in the periodical essay of which the *Spectator* can be taken as a standard. It included a fictional narrative of Sir Roger de Coverley and the members of his club, together with critical essays, prose fictions, sermons, epistles. Roy M. Wiles writes of the narratives of the *Spectator*, "In the 635 numbers there is an abundance of fables, moral tales, dreams, visions, allegories, and autobiographical letters." [67] To these should be added diaries, criticisms, arguments, and letters from correspondents. If one considers the *Spectator* with its varied fare and compares it with the periodical publication of Dickens' novels, one finds that Addison and Steele sought to contribute to an understanding of the world by addressing the different groups within it: "well-regulated families," "the fraternity of spectators," "the Blanks of Society," and the "female world" (*Spectator* 10). The aim of the periodical was "to make instruction agreeable" and "diversion useful" to the readers (*Spectator* 10). Dickens' view of his audience was more homogeneous, his fictions more tightly unified, his aim more consistent with the novel.

In the first number Addison identified the impartial character of the spectator with the concept of withdrawal as insight: by not participating in life one "can discern the errors in the economy, business and diversion of others, better than those who are engaged in them." The reason for this is that zeal is misleading. He related the diversity of his plan to political neutrality, the need to avoid party conflict. The diversity of forms was a way of providing a variety of interests that minimized the possibility of intense party commitment and violence. In *Spectator* 125 he wrote: "There cannot a greater judgment befal a country, than such a dreadful spirit of division as rends a government into two distinct people. . . ." [68]

If the periodical paper is seen as a combinatory form the purpose of which is to provide knowledge to a varied audience, to interest diverse groups, to reduce political pressures or factions,

[67] Wiles, "The Periodical Essay," pp. 22–23.
[68] *Works*, I, 308, 310.

one of the methods is to welcome participation of the audience by providing the possibility of cooperative authorship through letters to the *Spectator*. Another is to create multiple expectations by writing diverse essays that interrupt a series, such as the papers on *Paradise Lost* (267, 273, 285, 291, etc.) or *The Pleasures of the Imagination*.

The interrelation of forms served to foster a consciousness of interrelation of interests in readers. It suggested a mode of harmony that had as its implicit analogy God's variety. At the same time the interplay of forms helped reduce the rigidity of a literary hierarchy, for as subjects and languages were shared, the aims of the forms themselves grew more heterogeneous.

The primacy of didactic mixed forms has been identified with the awareness of religious and political factionalism. The hospitality to diversity, the desire to insist on proper discrimination or taste or decorum, the addresses to readers with instructions are all literary features that, by imitating human action, illustrated how diversity could or should be properly pursued. The principle of variety of features can thus be seen as corresponding to defenses of general principles of human nature by indicating the kinds of variations within any form.

The political underpinning of mixed forms necessarily gave to didactic works direct or indirect political implications. For Augustan writers and readers, these forms had to combine truth with fiction if their teaching was to be realized. The truth statements that combined with fictional narratives did not suddenly themselves become fictions. Because works were not indivisible wholes, truth and fiction could be related without being fused. Consider an example from the "Apology" to *A Tale of a Tub*. Swift writes, "The greatest Part of that Book was finished above thirteen Years since, 1696, which is eight Years before it was published." This is a true statement and all our additional evi-

dence supports it. When he writes, "In the Author's Original
Copy there were not so many Chasms as appear in the Book;
and why some of them were left he knows not," [69] this statement so far as we know is false. I have chosen two simple instances, but truth value was also to be found in an *Essay on Man*
with its moral and metaphysical precepts. And it was to be
found in Fielding's addresses to the reader. Truth statements
were a necessary part of didactic poems and could be found in
panegyric, elegy, most prose forms. Readers, therefore, were
addressed, challenged, guided, and goaded to discover the
proper distinctions, not because earlier theories had not made
them, but because mixtures had become so prevalent. The mixtures created a new kind of reader whose reading procedures undermined the overt statement about general human nature the
works contained.

This discussion of the Augustan concept of species has dwelt
on the critics' awareness of and the authors' practice of and the
readers' responses to genre mixtures and interrelations. And the
critics were not unaware of the individual responses they were
cultivating. In explaining that under the general title of hymns
were included many forms such as panegyrics, lyrics, and
elegies, as well as hymns, Bishop Lowth remarked that the clas-
sification of forms in the book of Psalms "is a matter dependant
[*sic*] in a great measure upon opinion, and not to be clearly demonstrated upon determinate principles; since the nature of the
subject, the complexion of the style, or the general form and
disposition of each poem, must decide the question; and [. . .]
different persons will judge differently upon these points.
. . ." [70] Their procedure was to assume that various combinations of features could be subsumed under the usual ends. But

[69] Swift, pp. 4, 17.   [70] Lowth, II, 144.

their statements about species and their practice of composition can only be made clear by an approach to genre that accounts for change synchronically as well as diachronically, by the nature of received forms and the alteration these undergo as a result of the commitment to mixtures, in this period, characteristic of didactic forms.

As the number of possible combinations of features increased in the course of the eighteenth century, the ends of the species began to change as well. Species criticism then ceased to provide the generalizations governing variety, generalizations necessary to explain how art provided models for mediation or meditation.

IV. SOME CONCLUSIONS

What are the implications of my thesis that neoclassical forms were mixed and interrelated, dominated by didactic models? With regard to the theory of genres, this view undermines the hypothesis that forms were pure or rigid. Some forms, like the epic and drama, were never considered "pure," and in the late seventeenth century the ideas of "purity" of form implied the removal of interrelations considered inappropriate, but appropriate interrelations were sanctioned.

The hierarchy that writers and critics of this period inherited from the Renaissance was altered in terms of the elevation of the longer didactic forms: the georgic, the epistle, and satire. But my argument is that the practice of all forms was infected by the didactic shift so that the elegy, lyric, ode, even drama and epic came to incorporate features of didactic forms or sometimes the forms themselves. Critics did not always agree on the propriety of such interrelations, but no critic denied that they existed.

The consequence of this for a theory of genre is that generic studies cannot be understood merely in terms of family traits or variation of a form studied diachronically. A genre is a part, at any period in literary history, of a family of forms. To study a form or genre one must grasp it in relation to other forms within the poetic hierarchy, just as one must understand prose forms— when no hierarchy exists—in terms of the principle of interrelation. This means that a genre course needs to be taught not merely in terms of a single kind, but of a hierarchy of kinds—for tragedy cannot be properly understood in its own traits or terms.

Critics referred and still refer to the principle of propriety or decorum and to the "rules" as a basis for judging the adequacy of any interrelation. These criteria were rooted in claims about the propriety of human relations and about the specific effects that works were to have upon readers or hearers at a particular time in history. The principle of interrelation, governed as it was by didactic procedures, altered the received effects by altering the means by which effects were achieved. Thus what needs to be emphasized is the freedom encouraged by the comparative critics and the procedures of interrelation. As the eighteenth century moved on, the justification of interrelations became a matter of the critic's acceptance or rejection of transitions, combinations, relation of part to whole. And these were inevitably tied to the critic's historical consciousness, his view of propriety as a comparative response to a modern reader's expectations.

The stipulation of "rules" was primarily cautionary and relative, urging writers not to take certain freedoms. But the interrelation of forms made such guides questionable, especially since the forms were part of a hierarchy not fully understood.

The implication of this thesis for interpretation is extensive. No literary work in the period can be understood without recognizing that it is a combination of parts or forms. This provides a basis for understanding "unity" as a *combination or interrelation of parts*. This unity will make it possible to relate a particular work to other works of the period. As I have demonstrated in regard to *A Tale of a Tub* and the *Spectator*, works that are considered disorganized or a series of discrete items can be seen as wholes in terms of the harmony of forms. Interpretation of eighteenth-century forms involves the recognition of features like allusion or mode as subsurface elements. Allusion draws attention to historical re-examination of a past work or passage or idea; mode involves the relation of a form like satire to its reduced function as part of another form. Such elements need to be compared to rhetorical procedures like repetition or antithetical parallelism that are available in other synchronic forms; these rhetorical procedures are parts of a common code in contrast to allusion or mode, which are parts of a different coding procedure. Combinations within a work permit different codes governed by the same procedures, but also different codes with different procedures.

The theoretical position of interrelation of forms and mixture of parts also leads to a view of language that combines two kinds of truth—referential and nonreferential—in the same work. Thus the idea of associative, composite, or combinatory forms requires the modern reader to adjust to depth as well as surface variations of language and to locate his selection of values within these rather than within the work as a self-reflexive whole.

Thus there becomes available a procedure for relating annotated forms like Latin poetry or English models to their parodies, such as *Tom Thumb* and *The Dunciad*. And forms not considered wholes—*Miscellanies*, periodical papers—can be understood as related by a common principle to the organization of literary forms contemporary with them.

Not only does this procedure widen the scope of what "literature" was considered to be, but it provides a basis for explaining
why a particular principle of interrelation was enacted or recognized. In terms of literary history, this common procedure provides a basis for period analysis, distinguishing the interrelations
of the late seventeenth and eighteenth centuries from those that
preceded and those that followed.

Such a hypothesis provides a systematic basis for dealing with
literary forms in all periods, and in doing so it takes account of
the continuity of forms and their interrelations, the changes that
occur in these forms, the introduction of new and the abandonment of old forms. And it is a hypothesis that explains more
works and more features within works than the premise of rigid,
distinct, and continuous genres that it supplants.

☙❦ RALPH W. RADER

The Concept of Genre and

Eighteenth-Century Studies

☙❦   THE subject of this paper is not genre in the prescriptive and conventional sense we associate with the eighteenth century itself, but rather a more fundamental conception
of genre that I believe needs to be made the basis of any poetics
capable of accounting for the realities of our literary experience.
But since our common subject here is the future of eighteenth-
century studies, I shall develop my views, with one exception,
entirely in terms of eighteenth-century examples and in
conclusion will suggest briefly some significant ways in which
adequate generic conceptions might improve and clarify not
only the formal but also the historical and cultural study of
eighteenth-century literature.

By and large modern critical theory and practice have not
seen generic distinctions as really significant. The main line of
modern criticism has tended to conceive poetry and all literary
structures as belonging in effect to a single genre, the genre of
statement. In this almost universally accepted view poetry is a

special kind of statement the meaning and value of which are to be identified with the peculiar syntactic and lexical structure alleged to be its vehicle.[1] This emphasis on the primacy of the sentence-statement seems to have developed originally as an attempt to defend the significance of literature against the threat posed by the reductive conceptions of meaning put forth with apparent authority by philosophers claiming to speak in the name of science. The arguments of these logical positivists—men like Carnap, Morris, and the early Wittgenstein—seemed to restrict meaning and truth value only to sentence statements meeting special conditions of logical form and empirical verifiability. Literary discourse, in such a view, had no significance at all, or at best an emotive one. The early theorists of the New Criticism—Ransom, Tate, and Brooks—following at a distance the lead of I. A. Richards, tacitly accepted the charge and attempted to turn the alleged defect of literary meaning into a virtue by asserting that the sentence-statements of literature were by their very nature not subject to the ordinary rules of language or logic or the claims of actuality; the freedom of literature from these bothersome restraints, in fact, somehow made it the "completest mode of utterance." [2] From such origins derives

[1] I have in mind here specifically Maynard Mack's statement in an influential article that "all poetry is in some sense poetry of statement" (" 'Wit and Poetry and Pope': Some Observations on His Imagery," *Pope and His Contemporaries: Essays Presented to George Sherburn*, ed. James L. Clifford and Louis A. Landa [New York, 1949], p. 20), but the idea is pervasive in modern criticism, as for instance in the notion that even novels are to be understood as expressing "themes."

[2] Perhaps the clearest example of this procedure is Allen Tate's criticism of the positivism of Charles W. Morris and the early Richards while effectively accepting the validity of the positivist analysis in his concept of a complex poetic "tension," a somewhat obscure notion in

the pervasive emphasis of modern criticism on the con-
tralogicality of poetic statement, its *lack* of meaning in the ordinary sense—upon irony, ambiguity, paradox, tension, texture,
metaphor, etc.; hence also the emphasis on its autonomy—its
formal disjunction from any external agency, reference, or intention—the concomitant doctrines of the intentional, biographical, and affective fallacies, and the development of the
concepts of the free-floating dramatic speaker and persona.

The price paid for this array of defensive armament has been
high, for these doctrines in effect deny semantic coherence to literary structures and eliminate the principle of excluded contradiction from critical discourse itself. Their use has therefore
made it possible to validate any desired interpretation of a literary work, however arbitrary, and brought us increasingly into a
situation in which, because literary works can be held to mean
nearly anything, they seem in effect to mean nothing at all.
Thus in defending literature its friends have inadvertently reduced it to the nonsense the positivists said it was and led some
recent critics actively to embrace the meaninglessness of literature as the sign of its profundity.

But it seems very likely now that the positivists were wrong—
premature and narrow, as Sir Karl Popper has shown, in their

---

which "extension" and "intension" are combined in a specially valid
semantic status, the precise nature of which Tate does not manage to
make clear. (See "The Present Function of Criticism," "Literature and
Knowledge," and "Tension in Poetry," collected with other essays in
On the Limits of Poetry [New York, 1948], esp. pp. 46–47 and 82–83.)
Tate's "tension," like Ransom's "texture," Brooks's "paradox," and
Empson's even more influential "ambiguity," all seem concepts deriving
in parallel fashion from Richards' own attempts to convert the terms of
his early reductive conception into a view of poetry in its special com-
plexities as the "completest mode of utterance."

notions even of scientific discourse,[3] and that in consequence the literary doctrines developed in reaction to them were also wrong. The positivist doctrine that all significant sentence-statements are to be understood as referring to or describing some empirical fact has been effectively challenged, from an orientation close to its own, by J. L. Austin and his followers, who have demonstrated that sentences in use express many kinds of significant acts beyond stating or describing. They may communicate judgments, threats, promises, commands and, in short, do all the things that men have always supposed they were able to do with language.[4] But speech act philosophy is only one of several disciplines which have indicated in recent years that the great and interesting task in the study of meaning is not to prescribe to man what he can know and how he should know but to try to gain some insight into the astonishing tacit

[3] On this matter see the 1958 Preface to Popper's *The Logic of Scientific Discovery* (New York, 1965), pp. 20–21 ("Unfortunately, there seems to be no such thing as the 'language of science' ") and the extended discussion of Carnap's philosophy offered by Popper in *Conjectures and Refutations: The Growth of Scientific Knowledge* (New York, 1968), particularly the section titled "Carnap and the Language of Science," pp. 264–73.

[4] See J. L. Austin, *How To Do Things with Words* (Oxford, 1962), and John R. Searle, *Speech Acts* (Cambridge, 1970). The basic semantic facts described by these philosophers were independently (and for literary analysis, more usefully) developed (in 1952) by Elder Olson in terms of his distinction between *lexis* and *praxis* in language. See his essay "William Empson, Contemporary Criticism and Poetic Diction," fully cited in note 6 below. (After this was written I encountered H. P. Grice's article "Utterer's Meaning and Intentions," *Philosophical Review*, 78 [April 1969], 147–77, which offers a view of meaning as determined by inferred intention significantly different from that of Austin and Searle and essentially similar, if I understand Grice's complex argument, to the one I employ below.)

FIGURE I

knowledge and means of tacit knowing that he already possesses but does not consciously understand or ordinarily even become aware of.[5]

An important general fact about the cognitive operations of the human mind is illustrated, I believe, by Figure 1, my version of the rabbit-duck which has been put to so many epistemological uses. Notice that it can be perceived either as a rabbit-like creature oriented toward the left or a duck-like creature oriented toward the right; notice also that it is impossible to

[5] The general processes of our "tacit knowing" have been extensively considered by Michael Polanyi, who seems to have originated the term. See Polanyi's *The Tacit Dimension* (New York, 1967) for a short introduction and, for fuller treatment, his *Personal Knowledge* (New York, 1964) and the essays collected in *Knowing and Being*, ed. Marjorie Grene (Chicago, 1969).

see it as both at the same time, that our perceptive apparatus
will not accept the ambiguity.[6] Why should this be? Most fundamentally and obviously, I think, because our minds have been
developed by evolution to enable us to operate in a world external to us which we must scan and interpret accurately and decisively if we are to survive. That we see any form at all in these
loose curves enclosing a dot clearly testifies to this meaning-seek-
ing faculty as does the fact that we are able to see the two things
we do see only alternately. The mind by its nature actively
seeks to impose meaning and to eliminate ambiguity in its encounters with the world,[7] and so it must certainly be also with
language.

[6] On the ambiguity of the rabbit-duck and visual ambiguity in general, see E. H. Gombrich's *Art and Illusion* (Princeton, 1960), pp. 5–7
and 232–41. The views Gombrich develops on the relation of ambiguity
to inferred intention and determining context serve to support the similar views advanced below about literature.

[7] In *The Senses Considered as Perceptual Systems* (Boston, 1966), J. J. Gibson shows that this assertion holds even at the level of sensory experience. Basing his argument on a comprehensive synthesis of the available
experimental evidence, Gibson demonstrates that the senses cannot be
adequately conceived as rigidly separated channels for the passive re-
ception of amorphous data but must be understood rather as coordi-
nated systems which actively seek out definitive information about the
structure of the environment in which they have been developed by
evolution to operate: "The activity of orienting and that of exploring
and selecting—the commonsense faculty of attending—is seen to be one
that extracts the external information from the stimulus flux while
registering the change as subjective feeling. . . . Perceptual development and perceptual learning are seen as a process of distinguishing the
features of a rich input, not of enriching the data of a bare and mean-
ingless input. *A perceptual system hunts for a state of what we call 'clarity'*
[my emphasis]. Whatever this state is physiologically, it has probably
governed the evolution of perception in the species, the maturation of
perception in the young, and the learning of perception in the adult" (p.

I mean by this that the mind in responding to a piece of language scans and interprets it so as to discover that meaning which renders the whole coherent and significant, to the exclusion of partial and incomplete meanings. In doing this the mind is pervasively dependent on the sort of interpretive assumptions about agentiality and intention that poetic theory has commonly proscribed as heretical. Take, for instance, the simple imperative sentence, "Close the door!" Considered in syntactical and lexical terms alone, the sentence might be said to have only one unequivocal meaning. Yet considered as a sentence in possible use it has a potentially infinite number of meanings. Consider if you will the different significances that one would assign to the sentence if it were uttered (1) by a man shivering from the effects of a draft; (2) by one man to another who had come in without closing the door; and (3) by a man who had been told that his long-estranged son was coming down the hall to see him. The effective differences in meaning could best be indicated by the use of three quite different sentences—something like "I'm cold!" in the first instance; "You're rude!" in the second; and "I don't want to see him" in the third. One might go on indefinitely making the sentence mean other things, but perhaps the essential point is clear: The interpreter of a sentence in use does not gather its meaning from the words taken in themselves, and he does not entertain all the meanings which the words separately and together might have; rather he assigns a

---

320). Gibson's radical but strongly confirmed hypothesis seems to contradict the basic assumptions of logical positivism and to support the view of Sir Karl Popper that human knowledge is not built up inductively from atomistic sense data but is developed rather as a chain of progressively refined hypotheses whose earliest source is the innate evolutionary endowment of the mind. (See Popper's *Conjectures and Refutations* [New York, 1965], p. 47.)

single coherent meaning by inferring intention, asking himself not, "What do these words mean?" but something like "What must the speaker mean to have used these words in this situation?" He asks himself this question and ordinarily gets his answer so rapidly that he is scarcely aware of the process, scarcely aware, without reflection, that the words in fact contain other possibilities of meaning.

Such facts as these, it seems to me, raise the strong presumption that the understanding we have of literature and the pleasure we take in it do not in fact derive from a reaction to specially literary disjunctions in the structure of the sentences themselves but, just the opposite, from a comprehensive inferential grasp of an author's overall creative intention in a work, which allows us to eliminate in the act of reading any potential incoherencies and ambiguities which cannot be resolved within our appreciation of the coherence of the whole.

The curious idea that literature, the highest use of language, involves ambiguous meanings floating free of intentional coherence to be gathered by the critic as he will is challenged by the most obvious facts of our everyday experience with language. I may illustrate this conveniently by an example which I have often used in teaching. In the motion picture "Up the Down Staircase," the heroine, a fledgling English teacher, begins her first class in a slum high school by writing on the board the line "There is no frigate like a book," whereupon the students burst into coarse laughter. The teacher does not intend and is not aware of the bawdy ambiguity which the class perceives in the unfamiliar word "frigate," and the class's instant and intuitive recognition of this fact is the basis of the laughter which they direct at her. Let us now imagine the same ambiguity employed in another situation. Let us imagine a man explaining the names of various kinds of ships to some dullard who keeps asking,

"What was the name of that one ship again?," whereupon the exasperated explainer replies, "I said *frigate!*" In this case an audience would automatically laugh *with* the speaker and *at* the questioner. The fact illustrated is known indubitably to us all: whether or not an ambiguity is registered as a virtue in expression is directly dependent upon whether or not it is judged to be intended, and this judgment is made by the hearer as an inherent part of his basic act of interpretation. It is indeed strange that this difference which in ordinary communication constitutes the difference between wit and foolishness should be obliterated by a dogma of criticism, as if ordinary men could make their significant intentions clear to us but poets could not.[8]

Let us now consider how the principle of interpretation according to inferred intention might bear upon a more complex piece of language. In an essay of characteristic force, Stanley Fish examines the sentence, "That Judas perished by hanging himself, there is no certainty in Scripture: though in one place it seems to affirm it, and by a doubtful word hath given occasion to translate it; yet in another place, in a more punctual description, it maketh it improbable and seems to overthrow it." Professor Fish's analysis of this sentence is a notable example of his

[8] The views expressed in the last two paragraphs have obviously been influenced by those put forth by Elder Olson in "William Empson, Contemporary Criticism and Poetic Diction," in *Critics and Criticism*, ed. R. S. Crane (Chicago, 1952), pp. 45–82, as my analysis of the New Critical position in general has obviously been influenced by essays in the same volume by Crane. But my views about the primacy and complexity of inferred intention are deliberately more radical than those of either Olson or Crane, and I have tried to make my conception of genre more comprehensive and more precise. I plan to discuss the relationship at greater length in a book on generic form now in progress, which will in part be an expansion of the materials of the present essay.

method, with which we are all familiar and which is a logical extension of the general New Critical position I have described. Professor Fish offers an analysis of the developing responses of the reader to the words as they succeed one another, as if the reader were conscious of and actively entertained all the meanings which the words at each stage of reading might *potentially* produce; and he emerges with the conclusion that this sentence, with its twists and turns and series of indefinite *it*'s, does not "yield a declarative statement," that it offers us "no information," but simply the experience of attempted but unsuccessful interpretation which is itself to be taken as the significance of the sentence.[9] That this analysis and conclusion are correct I do not believe. I do not believe that we read this or any other sentence in the piece-meal way Professor Fish suggests, taking the opportunity to go up as many semantic sidetracks toward dead ends as each segment of language considered independently might permit. If it were so, language would be of no more use to us than to the builders of Babel. Rather I believe that, even without a context, a reader reads this sentence (fairly easily) as he reads all sentences, by hypothesizing a comprehensive intention in terms of which the words make collective sense, to wit: "There is no certainty in Scripture that Judas perished by hanging himself. Though in one place it [Scripture] seems to affirm it [that he hanged himself], and by a doubtful word hath given occasion to translate it [that is, by a word of doubtful meaning in the original has prompted a translation which asserts that Judas hanged himself]; yet in another place, in a more punctual [that is, explicit] description, it [Scripture] makes it [the fact of hanging] improbable and seems to overthrow [that is, controvert] it [the fact of

_____

[9] See "Literature in the Reader: Affective Stylistics," *New Literary History*, 2 (Autumn 1970), 123–62; reprinted as an appendix to Fish's *Self-Consuming Artifacts* (Berkeley, 1972), pp. 383–427.

hanging]." With its meaning-oriented direction-finder, the mind gets through the tangle of references, emerging not with an experience of meaninglessness but with definite significance joined to a sense of inefficiency of expression. (We may notice, by the way, that the mind acutely attributes this inefficiency not to the ineptness of the writer, as it would with a sentence from a freshman composition, but to the development of English prose at the time the writer wrote.)

I return now to my suggestion above that the principle of inferred intention applies to literary as well as non-literary discourse. With literature too we understand by asking, "What must the author mean to have used these words?" or, more broadly and accurately, "What significant creative intention must I assume to make these words intelligible?" I substitute "creative intention" for "meaning" to avoid the implication that the sentences of literary works can be understood simply as "making statements" and to lay the basis for my full positive thesis. Though some literary works are properly understood as embodying statements—direct assertions of the author about the world in which we live—most use their sentences not to *assert* but, in different ways, to *represent*. They can be said to represent the activity of various kinds of real or imagined agents operating in various kinds of determinate relationship to the author for the sake of the various kinds of significance which such represented structures can have. Just as in our real-life examples language is intelligible only by reference to a significant intention inferred within a communicative situation, so in literary works the language is intelligible only in relation to the author's presumed intention to realize an inherently significant representational structure.

Such representational structures are identical with genre in the sense in which I am using the term, and they accord more or less well with the various generic categories—lyric, satire, essay, novel, history, etc.—commonly in use, except that common use does not involve a really analytic use of genre nor any recognition that generic structure is the primary determinant of intelligibility and value. Readers are always aware to some degree of making generic assumptions, and critics use them sometimes more, sometimes less explicitly in formulating critical interpretations. But just because generic features are structural, it is difficult for us to become fully conscious of their pervasive determination of intelligibility and effect; like all intuitively apprehended structures, they tend to remain covert. What I wish now to demonstrate is that the literary force of literary sentences does indeed arise from their placement within and contribution to the cognitive force field of the generic structure in which they are embedded and not atomistically and additively from any inherent character of their own as sentences. In order to illustrate at the same time some varieties of generic structure and the different kinds of cognitive operations the mind does in fact perform in its intuitive interpretations of them, I shall take as examples several eighteenth-century masterpieces—Gray's "Elegy," Goldsmith's "Deserted Village," and Johnson's "Vanity of Human Wishes," considered as a group together with "My Last Duchess," borrowed from the nineteenth century for reasons of explanatory convenience. I shall move then to a discussion of "The Rape of the Lock," and conclude with a brief comparative treatment of *Tom Jones* and Gibbon's *Decline and Fall.* I may point out here that all the poems, with the exception of the "Duchess," are quite similar in the kind of diction and syntax they employ and that all, with a minor rhyme variant in the "Elegy," are in iambic pentameter couplets—facts of linguistic similarity which point up the striking differences in imaginative experience offered by the poems.

To begin then with Browning's "Duchess," we may notice how vain is any effort to discover the source of its poetic effect in words and syntax taken by themselves. "That's my last duchess painted on the wall, / Looking as if she were alive. I call / That piece a wonder now," etc. We may compare this with my saying here, "That's my former colleague seated on the aisle, looking as if he were asleep." The difference in effect lies not in the slight difference of the words but in what Browning's words encountered on the page force us to postulate imaginatively in order to understand them.

It is a particularly clear illustration of my general point: as a cognitive necessity, *simply to render the words of the poem intelligible,* we must imagine the Duke as their agent, the gallery and the Duke's presence in it, the unknown auditor, and the Duke's as yet unrevealed purpose in speaking to him about the duchess and her portrait. The fourteen words of the opening sentence are a miracle of representational power, but so instantaneously is it performed that most readers accept the Duke's presence as a matter of no particular remark rather than as what it is, the central aesthetic fact of the poem. So vital has Browning made the Duke's presence, indeed, that critics often think of him as in effect the sole intelligence understood behind the words of the poem, almost as if he were in fact the real natural person he seems to our overt imagination. Such critics think of Browning's agency in the poem as something known or inferred extra-formally, outside the imagined experience of the poem. But a simple introspective test will show that this is not so. We may ask ourselves whether in reading we imaginatively hear the words of the poem as spoken by the Duke, and of course we reply that we do. We may then ask ourselves if we understand the rhymes that we hear in the poem as part of the Duke's speech, and we discover that we do not. This shows that prior

to any conscious analysis our imaginations register and respond
to the presence of two agents in the intuitive act of construing
the poem—a created actor, the Duke, and the immanent creator
Browning. The same imaginative fact can be shown by another
test. If we imagine the scene imaged in the poem as translated
into a cinematic medium—a useful imaginative test to
which I shall be resorting again—we shall discover that the
vividness and pleasure of the illusion would be sharply de-
creased, despite the great increment of visual particulars. The
reason for this is that the mind responds to the illusion as relative to the means used to produce it: it requires no art to project
an image of this drama as a motion picture of an actor duke
speaking the words of the poem to an actor emissary within a
scene visually actual to the eye; and the mind would not gain
enough re-creative pleasure from the mimetic process to entertain the image as vital illusion; but the delight of the lucid imitation through words alone is so great as to produce an illusion of
great intensity and beauty. But if this is so, again it must be that
the imagination registers and responds to the Duke not as an independent speaker but with a definite tacit awareness and appreciation of the fabricating poet behind him.

These considerations suggest that the concept of the autonomous dramatic speaker, of which the Duke is surely the
most unequivocal example, has generated so much critical confusion primarily because it is a highly oversimplified and explan-
atorily inadequate concept. A concept of greater explanatory accuracy and utility is the idea of a created agent best called an
"actor" (since he may or may not be a literal "speaker," as the
Duke is, but some other kind of agent) projected in specific formal relationship to an immanent poet. I shall be able to consider
fully only one more example of such a relationship, in Gray's
"Elegy," but before doing so I will remark in general that in my

view a prime source of difficulty with speaker-persona criticism has been a failure to distinguish adequately the many different kinds of specific functional relationships which such projective agents can have with the poet and a failure to see and consider the relationship as immanently defined by the poet. This failure to give adequate consideration to the controlling intention of the indwelling poet, though it reflects in part no doubt the inherent complexity of such imaginative constructions, derives in significant measure from a physicalist theory of language which has conceived sentences as mere sequences of sound symbols which could carry the meaning only of a single agent since only a single agent could utter them.

Turning now to Gray's "Elegy" we may notice that for the better part of two centuries it never occurred to anyone to suppose that the agent of the words in the poem was anyone but the poet Gray in his own proper person, but the interpretive possibilities opened up by modern theory have led some in recent years to the view that the speaker is to be entirely dissociated from Gray, is to be understood merely as a generalized dramatic Spokesman by any reader not perversely bent upon committing the biographical fallacy or violating the doctrine of the dramatically autonomous speaker.[10] Now there is in fact a clear intuitive basis for differentiating between Gray the poet and a second actor-agent of whom we are conscious in the poem, but this fact does not make the poem the dramatic monologue that the critics just alluded to hold it to be. The poet/actor relationship in the "Elegy" must be construed and responded to very differently from the poet/actor relationship in Browning's "Duch-

---

[10] Examples of such interpretations are conveniently available, with others, in *Twentieth Century Interpretations of Gray's "Elegy": A Collection of Critical Essays*, ed. Herbert W. Starr (Englewood Cliffs, N. J., 1968).

ess"; it must be construed in a way which, when fully concep-
tualized, complicates and enriches but essentially confirms, from
a strictly formal point of view, the old notion of the poem as an
expression of the biographical Gray. We may say that in the
"Elegy" as in the "Duchess" our imaginations respond to a fictive actor implicitly understood as created by a real poet: the
actor in the "Elegy" is the man in the churchyard at dusk; the
poet is the man who made the poem as an image of the man in
the churchyard. In the "Duchess," however, the Duke is
imagined as somatically external to the poet and us and is known
as another person is known, from the outside in, his inner self
inferred solely from external signs. The effect and significance
of our experience of him is like the effect and significance of
being the uninvolved completely absorbed observer of another
natural person whose inner purpose we apprehend through a
continuous act of sequential inference which, beginning in fo-
cused curiosity, ends in the satisfaction—and surprise—of full
knowledge.

In the "Elegy," by contrast, the churchyard actor is conceived
by the poet from within, so that we participate in his mental activity as if his eyes and his experience had become the poet's and
our own; and the effect and significance of his experience is registered in our consciousness as the effect and significance of our
own experience of the external world is registered. That this formal contrast between the two poems is accurate as a matter of
objective imaginative fact we may demonstrate to ourselves by
transposing the experience of the two poems into cinematic
terms. We will see the Duke as an outward presence within the
frame of the motion picture screen, gesturing and speaking the
words of the poem, whereas with the "Elegy" we will see the
scene of the churchyard landscape with the camera imaginatively understood to be the actor's eyes through which we are

looking and with the words of the poem registered as the "voice over" projection of the actor's inward stream of meditation with which we are identified. A related confirmational test of the objectivity of the imaginative contrast is a simple reading aloud of the two poems: the reader will discover that he projects the Duke's voice dramatically as characterizing the "otherness" of the Duke, but that the voice of the "Elegy" will be an ideal extension of the reader's own voice. Such imaginative facts as these, when they can be unequivocally asserted as universal, constitute very powerful tests for any literary theory with claims to empirical validity.

These considerations directly illuminate, I believe, the intuitive basis of the common reader's automatic reference to the actor in the poem as "Gray," though it is also clear that the figure in the poem is imaginatively distinct from Gray, as already specified.[11] In fact a great deal of our pleasure in this poem as in the "Duchess" derives from our intuitive appreciation of their conjoint agency. Consider, for instance, our response to the single word "glimmering" from the line "Now fades the glim-

[11] The definite but quite different ways in which intuition permits the poet's name to be related to his agent in various kinds of dramatic poems does not bear out the doctrine that such agents are uniformly detached and autonomous. In dramatic monologues like "My Last Duchess," as already indicated, the agent is emphatically "other" than the poet and never confused with him, whereas the agents in "Dover Beach" and "The Windhover," like the agent in the "Elegy," can casually be referred to as "Arnold" or "Hopkins" without drawing protest from an undergraduate class (or even more sophisticated critics), though consideration of the dramatic representation will always produce qualification of this response. In sharp contrast, the agents in "Tintern Abbey" and *In Memoriam must* be referred to as "Wordsworth" and "Tennyson." These differences seem to betoken important generic distinctions.

mering landscape on the sight." Our total apprehension of the "significance" of the word is a combination of seeming to see the landscape as the actor sees it in the visually unsteady light of the dusk and our implicit simultaneous appreciation of the aesthetic loveliness of the poet's act of mimesis as he stretches the sight-symbolic word "glimmering" over two metrical feet, using the rippling anapest of the second foot as a verbal correlative of the wavering light.

Poet and actor in the "Elegy" are clearly related then not in the mode of the dramatic monologue but of the dramatic lyric, to use the contrastive terms so brilliantly developed by Robert Langbaum,[12] and it is perhaps worthwhile to say a word more about our assumption of the effective consubstantiality of the poet and actor as characteristic of the dramatic lyric. I believe the assumption derives not only from the imaginative features specified above, but also from our intuitive recognition that that actor, dramatically independent though he is, was built out of a memory of the poet's, that the experience we share with the actor has the character of an artificial re-creation and/or ex-trapolation of an experience which the poet did not invent.[13] This hypothesis would explain the complex sense of artifice and actuality we have in such poems, and it contributes incidentally to a solution of what has been the most puzzling crux in Gray's poem—the problem of why the "me" of line four addresses him-self as "thee" in line ninety-three and then proceeds to supply

[12] In *The Poetry of Experience: The Dramatic Monologue in Modern Literary Tradition* (New York, 1963).

[13] If the reader attempts to explain the artistic rationale of the choice of Dover Beach as the setting for Arnold's dramatic lyric, he may be surprised to discover that he has assumed that the experience represented in the poem was not invented and assigned to Dover Beach but in fact took place there. Similarly, though we have no knowledge that Hopkins was ever enraptured by the sight of a windhover at dawn, no reader would be surprised if a letter turned up recording such an experience.

himself in a roundabout fashion with an imagined epitaph which
an imagined rustic might in the future invite the reader to read.
The greater Romantic lyric as described by M. H. Abrams was
not yet coherently in being, its full lyrical form only beginning
to take shape in Gray's and other hands. Gray moved away in
the course of the poem from the explicitly dramatic representation of the actor's lyrical response to the initial setting and situation toward a more generalized meditation appropriate to
eighteenth-century conventions and proceeding more and more
as if from the "real I" of the didactic poet. But the meditation
was in fact developed to be an organic part of the lyrical action,
as is shown by Gray's abrupt attempt in the abbreviated first
version of the Eton manuscript to conclude the poem not with a
generalization but with a resolution, derived from the churchyard meditation, of the actor's specific personal problems:

> And thou, who mindful of the unhonour'd Dead
> Dost in these Notes their artless Tale relate
> By Night and lonely Contemplation led
> To linger in the gloomy Walks of Fate
>
> Hark how the sacred Calm, that broods around
> Bids ev'ry fierce tumultuous Passion cease
> In still small Accents whisp'ring from the Ground
> A greateful Earnest of eternal Peace
>
> No more with Reason & thyself at Strife;
> Give anxious Cares & endless Wishes room
> But thro' the cool sequester'd Vale of Life
> Pursue the silent Tenour of thy Doom.

Looking back one sees that from the first the experience represented in the poem is implicitly shaped so as to justify the actor's positive acceptance of a life of obscurity leading through

death to eternal peace. But Gray had a problem. Though he had recreated with complete lucidity the impact of the churchyard experience which had ignited in him the train of thought developed in the poem, he had not represented the continuing personal conflict out of which it had arisen, so that the references, in the original Eton manuscript ending, to his ambition, his strife with reason and himself, as well as the admonition to pursue his silent doom, seem quite unprepared for and aesthetically inert. The conflict was the poet's in his own proper person, and the attempt to assign it to the actor, his lyrical projection, by addressing him as a "thou" who is writing the poem, though it was a way back from the apparent disengagement of the didactic I, was clearly an external assertion not formally organic with the imaginative reality of the actor, which is figured for the reader entirely in terms of his presence in the churchyard. But, it must have seemed to Gray, there was no other way to bring in and resolve the conflict which made sense of it all; especially after the didactic disjunction, there was no way to build the conflict dramatically into the actor's response to the stimulus of the churchyard. This difficulty seems to account for Gray's long delay in completing the poem, but at last he must have hit upon the brilliant if slightly confusing device of projecting (through the "hoary-headed Swain") a merely hypothetical future for the actorial "thou" which could be represented entirely in terms of the graveyard established as the basis of imaginative probability in the poem. In this way, the pre-existent conflict, merely asserted in the original ending, could be fully and harmoniously expressed through the figure of the actor and, in the epitaph, beautifully resolved. By the same means he was able to achieve the effect of special decorum, so finely elucidated by Bertrand H. Bronson, of presenting with dignified obliquity the extremely personal sentiments embodied in the imagined epitaph.[14] But we could not appreciate the delicacy of this obliquity at all if we did not intuitively apprehend that the poet Gray and the actor of the poem were effectively identical. And so, returning to the main line of my thesis, we see that in reading the "Elegy" at least commission of a sophisticated version of the biographical fallacy is a formal necessity.

In "The Deserted Village" Goldsmith, writing after the example of Gray's poem, encounters a similar problem in inverted form. Where Gray's movement toward apparent meditation was really lyric, Goldsmith's genuinely didactic poem sprang from such deep personal sources that it verged toward lyric, and, like the "Elegy," demanded a special formal solution. All of Goldsmith's formal choices develop his poem steadily in the direction of didactic generality. The opening apostrophe, with its poignant evocation of Auburn's vanished charms, is immediately followed by a prospective statement of the moral ("Ill fares the land," etc.) and then a generalization of the Auburn situation to all of England (ll. 57–74). Only when the overall didactic course of the poem is thus firmly set does Goldsmith develop the sense of lyric presence at the site of the depopulated village ("Here as I take my solitary rounds") and indicate the background of personal suffering which stands behind and implicitly energizes the whole creative act of the poem: In a world of long vexation where strong temptations fly, "Remembrance wakes . . . and turns the [far-off childhood] past to pain." Despite the fact that

[14] See Bronson's "On a Special Decorum in Gray's Elegy," reprinted in his *Facets of the Enlightenment* (Berkeley and Los Angeles, 1968), pp. 153–58. The argument of the whole paragraph is essentially a translation of the substance of Bronson's analysis into generic terms, so that where he emphasizes the peculiar structure of the "Elegy" as resulting from the poet's sense of personal decorum, I see it more as the consequence of a potential formal impasse in the poem.

the lyric element is itself immediately generalized (ll. 97ff.), we respond to the loving reconstruction of lost Auburn which follows as supporting the public thesis primarily through the sense it communicates of private loss. The imaginary vision is nonetheless strongly followed by a translation of the private significance of the memories into a base for a generalized articulation of the theme, concluding with the encapsulating line, "The country blooms—a garden and a grave." This is followed by a likewise general contemplation of the lot of the expropriated peasantry which is midway neatly transposed into an account of the specific fate of the Auburn folk in the fearful "distant climes" of Georgia. By this means Goldsmith resolves the expectations attached to the development of the general theme and also those independently raised by the representation of Auburn. (The general and specific exodus had been explicitly foreshadowed in ll. 50 and 73 respectively.) Left unresolved at this point is the sense of personal fate attached to the voice of the poem as grounded in the present landscape of the village. On the one hand the voice never achieves the simulated somatic autonomy of the actor in the "Elegy" but is a mere device for the intensified expression of the theme; on the other hand, as already suggested, it is registered as attached to an emotion which is not subordinate to the didactic intention of the poem but which rather exists prior to and generates it. The voice proceeds from a stylized presence behind which the reader senses the poet, as behind the stylized Auburn he senses what is in fact Lissoy. The burden of this presence demanded discharge but could not be resolved within the merely internal terms of the representation, which would themselves be satisfied merely by the renewed conjunction of the thematic material with the landscape-located voice: "Even now, methinks, *as pondering here I stand,* / I see the rural virtues leave the land." The one means of complete resolution was for Goldsmith himself to enter the poem in the only role available, as poet; but a stage-center presentation of himself in his substantive identity would have broken the representational facade and dissipated the force of the didactic message. Goldsmith's solution was the address to a personified Poetry which permitted first the (subordinated) expression of the emotion externally attached to his poetic role and then an easy transition back to an assertion of his internal poetic theme ("Teach erring man," etc.), in which the full personal voice is climactically conflated with the public message. Even so, Goldsmith was not himself able to carry this design completely through and accepted finally from Johnson the lines which brought the poem to the emphatic, purely didactic conclusion which the overall form required.

Taken together, the formal problems which developed for Gray in the "Elegy" and for Goldsmith in "The Deserted Village" suggest a larger conflict in the eighteenth century between external didactic norms and the internal logic of the emerging dramatic lyric and, I believe, other genres also, as well as a general means by which historical developments within a given genre might be conceived and analyzed.

The overt message of the four strong lines which Johnson provided for Goldsmith's poem reminds us that his own powers were best suited to the kind of poetry exemplified in "The Vanity of Human Wishes," a poem quite properly called a poem of statement since it requires us to assume only the "real I" agency of the poet and an intention to establish, by argument and example, a truth bearing on the conduct of life. But even in this poem, as in poems of similar structure by Pope and others, meaning, effect, and value depend not on syntax and diction considered in themselves but as they are made to realize the mental and moral power of the author in his objectified persuasive act. And of course the "statements" embodied in such a poem can be as empirical, as indubitably true as our sense of life itself: "From Marlb'rough's eyes the streams of dotage flow, / And Swift expires, a driv'ler and a show." Merely in conceiving the examples our imagination assents to the thesis of the poem and finds its beauty in the austere brevity with which they are adduced.

Critical discussions of "The Rape of the Lock" usually place emphasis on local rhetorical effects and/or large perspectives loosely derived from literary or religious tradition as these are held to bear in a general evaluative way on Belinda and the social world of which she is a part. Valuable as much of this criticism has been, it has seldom attempted to explain either the concrete imaginative force of the work or its large structual features as deriving from Pope's attempt to realize a specific overall satiric intention.

I mean by satire a work whose intelligibility and value is determined by a formally embodied intention to ridicule an object understood to exist outside the work.[15] It is a work designed to make fun of something or someone, and if there is nothing there to be made fun of, there is no meaning and pleasure for the reader. The triangular psychic mechanism embodied in satire is closely analogous to that described by Freud as essential to the tendentious joke: "Generally speaking, a tendentious joke calls for three people: in addition to the one who makes the joke, there must be a second who is taken as the object of the hostile or sexual aggressiveness, and a third in whom the joke's aim of

[15] The notion of satire as directing ridicule against a target existing outside the work itself is conventional, though its full analytical implications are seldom developed. My own use of the term assumes the rigorous working out of the concept offered by Sheldon Sacks, *Fiction and the Shape of Belief* (Berkeley and Los Angeles, 1964), pp. 5–12 and 31–49.

producing pleasure is fulfilled." [16] In satire, in parallel, we have the author who is understood as constructing the satiric fiction as a means of ridiculing a real human target for the pleasure of the spectator reader.

We understand then that when, in teaching "The Rape of the Lock," we all as an automatic preliminary tell the story of Arabella Fermor, Lord Petre, and the ravished lock, we do so to fill out and clarify the immanent basis of intelligibility everywhere implied in the poem, most obviously in the line, "This, ev'n Belinda may vouchsafe to view," which makes sense only on the assumption that Belinda has an external counterpart conscious of and responsive to the poet's representation of her in the poem. This assumption on the reader's part is the basis of significance and effect throughout.

The pervasive external reference of the "Rape" is tacitly recognized by critics who emphasize the primacy of Pope's "attitude toward Belinda" but who perhaps do not consciously perceive that the reference is necessarily intuited as external because the details of the fiction, except for the cutting off of the lock itself, have no manifest real-world counterparts, a fact which logically might seem to make the story functionally a fiction independent of fact. But the formal situation involved is exactly parallel to that of a journalistic satire in our own day by a Buchwald or a Hoppe, where one real event—a presidential decision, say—is used as the basis of a dramatic sketch manifestly fictional and yet understood as meaningful and emotionally effective only in relation to the initially given real-world fact.

In order to account for the peculiar structural features of "The

[16] Sigmund Freud, *Jokes and Their Relation to the Unconscious*, ed. James Strachey (New York, 1963), p. 100.

Rape of the Lock," we need to define its precise satiric intention. In the special quality of its ridicule the "Rape" stands at the opposite end of the satiric spectrum from Swift's Book Four. Where Swift seeks to vex and not at all to divert the reader by making him at once the witness and (through his participation in human nature) the object of attack, both the second and third persons of Freud's triangle, Pope's purpose is best defined as an intention to ridicule as a fault the excesses of Belinda's reaction to the loss of her lock but to do so in the most flattering and pleasing way consistent with its still appearing to be a fault. The reader's pleasure in the poem derives from his knowing complicity in the benevolent fun being made of Belinda, his appreciation of the easy readiness of invention and bland urbanity of manner with which the poet makes good everywhere his pretence, at once flattering and reductive, to take Belinda's vanity more seriously than she does herself, to create in his shimmering fiction its objective correlative, transparently false but mimetically indubitable. Where others might see merely a vain girl with her nose in the air, Pope reveals her justification in a dazzling retinue of invisible sylphs. Where others might say that Belinda had unbecomingly lost her temper, Pope describes it all with straight face as resulting entirely from the machinations of Umbriel and his visit to the Cave of Spleen, things for which Belinda obviously cannot be blamed. (Anyway, it is not Belinda but Thalestris who speaks the words of Belinda's anger.) Even when in 1717 it seems necessary to add a moral to make Belinda's fault a little more definite, Pope certainly does not place it in the usual place for morals, in unflattering emphasis at the end, nor even offer it in his own voice. Rather, with artful ventriloquism, he gives it obliquely, through Belinda's enemy, Clarissa, at the beginning rather than the end of the last canto. There, of course, he had already, in 1712, offered his assurance that the lock had risen to the glory of a star, though seen, to be sure, only by his own "quick, poetic eyes." What beautiful final fun to make of Belinda's overevaluation of her lost lock, but there it still is, at the poem's end, shining in immortal flattery.

Since I have dealt here only with structural features usually neglected in analysis, I shall indicate briefly how, as with the "Elegy," the generic principle informs not only the large features but the smallest particularities of diction as well. If we consider, for instance, the single word "appears" in the line "A heav'nly Image in the Glass appears," we see that its force derives from the lucidity with which it conveys at once the fiction of the mystical apparition of deity and the correlated literal fact of the instantaneous materialization of Belinda's reflection in the mirror which speciously justifies the poet's pretense to believe his fiction. The same fact holds for, "To that she bends, to that her Eyes she rears"—a simultaneous rendering of the fictive acts of worship and the literal movements of primping—as well as for all the other often-appreciated *double entendres* of this magical passage. (It is worth noticing in passing that the double references of the passage are sometimes referred to as "metaphorical," whereas they are more properly described as merely the local manifestation of the satiric fictional surface which throughout overlays the representation of the literal satiric target beneath; the passage is metaphoric in the same sense that the sylphs and the Cave of Spleen are metaphoric, not in a general poetic way, but in a way peculiar to satiric structures.) [17]

I have meant in this analysis to show the critical power of

[17] Though I do not entirely agree with the concept of satire as a genre put forth by Edward W. Rosenheim, Jr., in his *Swift and the Satirist's Art* (Chicago, 1963), I have nevertheless been influenced by his arguments and particularly by the concept of "satiric fiction" as advanced on pp. 17–23 and elsewhere.

considering satire in terms of unifying generic intention rather
than through local rhetorical devices and/or allusive contexts,[18]
but one final point may be necessary to make my conception of
satire fully clear and protect me from an obvious criticism.
Though I hold that a work like "The Rape of the Lock" must be
imaginatively construed as attacking an object outside itself and
therefore located in time, I do not conceive the value of the
greatest of such works to be limited by their time-bound reference. The permanent quality of such poems depends on two fac-
tors: (1) the degree of aesthetic perfection with which the satiric
act of the poet is embodied in the work; and (2) the degree to
which a knowledge of the external object adequate to a full
response is internally inferable from the work itself. "The Rape
of the Lock" is the greatest and most continuingly vital of our
verse satires because it fully meets both of these conditions.
"Absalom and Achitophel," on the other hand, though a construction of great aesthetic power, has not so vital a continuing
life because of its weakness in respect to the second condition.

Before concluding I have time to offer two brief final examples of generic analysis, one of a novel, one of a history—*Tom
Jones* and Gibbon's *Decline and Fall*, examples also used in a
recent study which badly blurs what I believe is a polar contrast
in intelligibility and value between fictive and factual narratives.[19] I have elsewhere taken the position, not obvious even to

[18] Our pleasure in the epic allusions of the poem and its adherence to
epic conventions derives not, as is often implied, from their "meaning"
taken in some loosely ideational way but from our perception of the in-
genuity and brilliance of the poet's adaptation of them to his precise satiric needs. The same kind of confusion of agent-of-ridicule with ve-
hicle-of-meaning lies beneath much of the controversy concerning Book
Four of *Gulliver's Travels*. See Sacks, *Fiction and the Shape of Belief*, p. 11.

[19] I refer to Leo Braudy's *Narrative Form in History and Fiction* (Princeton, 1970). Braudy does not totally override the distinction between

some quite sophisticated critics, that true stories and fictitious stories differ not only in their extrinsic relationship to the real world but in their intrinsic imaginative structure, which invites and requires the assumption of factuality or fictionality, as the case may be, to be properly understood and responded to.[20] I have argued further that factual works which achieve the status of literary masterpieces raise the essential fact they offer us out of hypothetical existence and display it to our imaginations as inherently true in the act of conception and inherently valuable because of some permanent relevance to human nature and/or some universal aspect of the human situation.[21]

The experienced value of Gibbon's work depends very much

---

fiction and history, but he seems at times to come close to it, as when he builds upon Fielding's reference to his works as "histories" an illegitimate comparison of the problems and methods of the two modes (pp. 91 ff.) or makes such a statement as: "He [Fielding] defines in the narrator of *Tom Jones* the model historian who constructs from the materials of observation, learning, and authority an appropriate causal pattern, without necessity but with plausibility, and totally fitted to the varied world in which we must live" (p. 180). Having moved fiction toward fact, Braudy moves fact toward fiction, emphasizing that Gibbon "shapes and gives meaning to history" (p. 257) as opposed to the possibility that Gibbon discovers and represents a particular objective aspect of historical truth. Much of Braudy's analysis of Gibbon's shaping presence in his history is accurate and valuable, but it is achieved at the expense of under emphasizing the factual authenticity of its effect, as the whole argument of Braudy's book is developed at the expense of obscuring a fundamental and analytically essential generic distinction.

[20] My argument on this point is developed most fully in my essay "Defoe, Richardson, Joyce, and the Concept of Form in the Novel" in *Autobiography, Biography, and the Novel* (Los Angeles, 1973). See also the essay cited in the succeeding footnote.

[21] See my "Literary Form in Factual Narrative: The Example of Boswell's *Johnson*" in *Essays in Eighteenth-Century Biography*, ed. Philip B. Daghlian (Bloomington, Ind., 1968), pp. 3–42.

upon our sense that the events it treats were not invented but, in
Carlyle's phrase, "did in very fact occur." Gibbon has recorded
the "strong emotions" which agitated his mind as he first ap-
proached and entered Rome and told how, "after a sleepless
night," he "trod with a lofty step" the ruins of the Forum: "each
memorable spot where Romulus stood, or Tully spoke, or Caesar fell, was at once present to my eye; and several days of in-
toxication were lost or enjoyed before I could descend to a cool
and minute investigation." It was a few days later, "as I sat mus-
ing amidst the ruins of the Capitol, while the bare-footed fryars
were singing vespers in the Temple of Jupiter, that the idea of
writing the decline and fall of the city first started to my mind."
The giant fragments of magnificence before him must have led
his imagination outward in space and backward in time and
forced it to an overwhelming inference of the past grandeur of
the empire at the same moment that they bore most eloquent
witness to the fact of its ruin. His history may be considered an
image constructed to be objectively adequate to the knowledge
and consequent emotion arising from that moment of grand sur-
mise. In reading the book, as we watch emperor succeed emperor, grand hopes arise, desperate ambitions lapse; as wave
after wave of barbaric incursion is followed by repulse, stabiliza-
tion, absorption, and new incursion; as century yields to century and the very substance of the empire shifts, dissolves, and
reconstitutes itself beneath the names and images of its institutions and traditions, we come to grasp what Gibbon grasped and
what we could never otherwise have imagined—the stupendous
magnitude of the Empire and how infinitely beyond individual
understanding and control the long oscillating process of it was.
The effect of Gibbon's history depends not as we might casually
suppose upon any intricate explanatory truths he offers, or upon
the validity of an overall "theory of history," but simply upon

the indubitable image he makes of some primal facts: that the Roman Empire was a grand and awesome human achievement, that it passed out of existence, and that those living during its decline—"the greatest, perhaps, and most awful scene in the history of mankind"—were neither aware of it, nor able, if they had been, to prevent it. ("It was scarcely possible that the eyes of contemporaries should discover in the public felicity the latent causes of decay and corruption.") The history offers in sum a deeply moving factual image of the proud resilience with which a high civilization maintained its massive life against the blind forces of dissolution: "The decline of Rome," Gibbon says, "was the natural and inevitable effect of immoderate greatness. Prosperity ripened the principle of decay; the causes of destruction multiplied with the extent of conquest; and as soon as time or accident had removed the artificial supports, the stupendous fabric yielded to the pressure of its own weight. The story of its ruin is simple and obvious; and instead of inquiring *why* the Roman empire was destroyed, we should rather be surprised that it subsisted so long."

Concurrently with his perception of the grand spectacle the reader is offered empathetic participation in the counterpoising act of the lucid intellect which conceives it all. Gibbon's measured irony and urbane detachment, reflecting his commitment to the most characteristic values of the civilization he memorializes, imply as well his recognition and deep acceptance of his own and the collective fate. (Gibbon tells his story throughout with the almost melancholy languor of one who, like Eliot's Tiresias, has foreseen and foresuffered all—as indeed he had at the ruins of the capitol—and is therefore beyond enthusiasm or surprise.)

Whereas in a fictional work the intention to produce an emotional effect precedes and shapes narrative substance, in a factual work emotional effect rises out of and completes the apprehension (as true) of an aspect of objective fact. The factual artist must reveal, not fabricate, the object of emotion, or the effect is lost. In Gibbon's work the effect is left to emerge unbidden from the overall construction of the facts but at crucial points is brought to explicit expression. In his first paragraph, for instance, Gibbon begins by locating the empire in the past and evoking its grandeur—"In the second century of the Christian era, the empire of Rome comprehended the fairest part of the earth and the most civilized portion of mankind. The frontiers of that extensive monarchy were guarded by ancient renown and disciplined valour. The gentle but powerful influence of laws and manners had gradually cemented the union of the provinces"—goes on at once to register with unbroken syntactical calm the seeds, then unperceived, of inevitable decay— "Their peaceful inhabitants enjoyed and *abused* the advantages of wealth and luxury. The *image* of a free constitution was preserved with *decent* reverence: the Roman senate *appeared* to possess the sovereign authority and devolved on the emperors all the executive powers of government"—and returns to the full note of civilized felicity before striking, with restrained but reverberating force, the pendant and climactic chord of incipient tragedy: "During a happy period of more than fourscore years, the public administration was conducted by the virtue and abilities of Nerva, Trajan, Hadrian, and the two Antonines. It is the design of this and of the two succeeding chapters to describe the prosperous condition of their empire, and afterwards, from the death of Marcus Antoninus, to deduce the most important circumstances of its decline and fall, a revolution which will ever be remembered and is still felt by the nations of the earth."

The formal principle becomes likewise explicit in the opening sentences of the famous chapters on Christianity: "A candid but rational inquiry into the progress and establishment of Christianity may be considered as a very essential part of the history of the Roman empire. While that great body was invaded by open violence, or undermined by slow decay, a pure and humble religion gently insinuated itself into the minds of men, grew up in silence and obscurity, derived new vigor from opposition, and finally erected the triumphant banner of the Cross on the ruins of the Capitol." The latter sentence (a close equivalent of Gibbon's initiating experience) reindicates the pervasive fact of the empire's magnitude ("that great body"), notes unconcerned the cooperating cancers of external and internal barbarism, and with serene irony creates the subjective victory of rational civilization in the antithesis which marks its objective defeat at the hands of superstition.

The meaning, beauty, and value of Gibbon's narrative then depend upon its truth as realized to the reader's imagination. Just as clearly the meaning, beauty, and value of *Tom Jones* depend on its fictionality, on the reader's appreciation of the fact that the shape of events presented to his imagination has been constructed, not reported, by the author. In another essay I have argued that the general novel form described by R. S. Crane, after Aristotle, in terms of the concept of "action" (of which *Tom Jones* is a comic sub-type) is, in effect, an objective fantasy, since its structural rationale is the pleasurable resolution of a dynamically developed tension deriving from the reader's induced wishes for a character's fate as compared with his induced expectations.[22] In such novels our sense of reality is (more or less fully and deeply) accommodated to the pressure of our

---

[22] See the essay cited in n. 18 above, pp. 33–34; R. S. Crane, "The Concept of Plot and the Plot of *Tom Jones*," *Critics and Criticism*, pp. 616–47; and Sheldon Sacks, *Fiction and the Shape of Belief*, pp. 15–20 and elsewhere.

wishes, values, and beliefs. In *Tom Jones* specifically we respond
to the author's direction of our desires and expectations for
Tom, so that in the end what we had wished for him against the
appearances of a world only seemingly like the random real one
we inhabit, comes miraculously to pass, as the world of apparent reality becomes the world of realized desire. The world of
Tom Jones is, then, fundamentally a world of wish, of hope, of
(in its specific case) rehearsal of providential faith. The most
fundamental source of this providential sense is the fact that
those actions of Tom which establish his desert are also understood as the necessary but not sufficient cause of his coordinate good fate, so that the lines of coincidence which lead to that
fate are accordingly registered as finally determined by transcendent agency. " 'The Lord disposeth all things,' " says Allworthy, and in the book we participate in the pleasing illusion
that He does, within a more fundamental awareness that it is
Fielding who contrives it all.[23] The Fielding-Gibbon contrast illustrates as well as I can in a short space my contention that the
more explicitly and precisely our experience of fictive and factual stories is analyzed, the more clearly it appears that they are,
as common sense would suppose, polar in structure and significance.

[23] The notion that *Tom Jones* incorporates as a peculiar dimension of
the reader's satisfaction a sense of the operation of supernatural agency
within the events of the book has been remarked upon by Dorothy Van
Ghent, *The English Novel: Form and Function* (New York, 1953), pp.
78–79, and by Wayne Booth, *The Rhetoric of Fiction* (Chicago, 1961), p.
217. Robert Wess offers the most rigorously formal account of the origin of this sense in the novel in his fine article "The Probable and Mar-
vellous in *Tom Jones*," *MP*, 68 (1970), 32–45; and in my unpublished dissertation "Idea and Structure in Fielding's Novels" (Indiana University,
1958), I trace out the Providential pattern in detail and relate it to its
conceptual basis in the doctrines of the Latitudinarian divines.

Moving now toward conclusion I may remark that if many of my observations on the works discussed here seem obvious, I make no apology, since they ought to seem so if they are indeed as I have claimed merely an explicit and systematized articulation of an intuitive understanding of literary structures which we all possess as a potential dimension of our natural cognitive capacity. But if my observations and their theoretical basis are even something like the truth, it would seem likely that the main line of contemporary literary study has gone harmfully wrong, not of course in its best practice, but in fostering a theory which permits and even encourages irresponsible critics to distort and override the native limits of significance in literary structures. Such a theory in effect exempts critical assertion from the principles of logic and the standards of meaning which are the necessary conditions of significant argument, so that, as I initially observed, by permitting literature to mean anything, such a theory leaves it in effect meaning nothing. By contrast the kind of theoretical view for which I have argued does not conceive literature as characterized by a special syntax and a coordinate plurisignation upon which the critic may ring whatever semantic changes he will, but as a system of structures, self-intelligible and self-justifying, which, through their embodiment in language, are developed and comprehended by imaginative extension of the mind's inherent capacity to grasp and respond to the world of which it is a part.

Such a theoretical point of view suggests also a significant reversal of emphasis in our understanding of the interdependence of the values embodied in literature and those values associated with the religious beliefs and myths of the past. In our nostalgia for the grand faiths of traditional Western culture, for its spiritual splendors and the dignity, reflecting the Great Chain of Being, supposedly attached to its hierarchical social structure, we have been led too easily to conceive the experienced value of the literary work as if it were in fact identical with an external structure of value once vitally located—and now lost—in the past, whereas the view outlined here would emphasize value as inhering in the embodied cognitive act of the work itself and see in it our most vital means of access to whatever in the values of the past was truly valid and universal.

More particularly as concerns the historical study of literature, a generic approach would encourage students to conceive more accurately the specific nature of the literature of a particular historical period, the eighteenth century in our present view. Rather than emphasizing exclusively the homogeneities that have indeed been shown to pervade the century's literature—its tendency toward generality, clarity, and simplicity, toward overt formality and stylization, toward didacticism; its preoccupation with classical models, conventions, and traditions—a richer kind of historical analysis could be produced through an endeavor to discover precisely how such homogeneities are brought into creative relationship with differing kinds of generic structure, how different forms are differently adjusted to the larger lines of cultural force. Attention could also be paid to the problem of why certain genres flourish at certain times—why for instance the great achievements of the early eighteenth century should be in satire, of the mid-century in the novel, of the late century in factual prose.

Most significantly of all perhaps generic concepts could be combined with historical studies in an attempt to write a genuine literary history, a history that would attempt to understand the processes involved in the invention and development of generic forms in themselves, the kind of history, envisaged by the late R. S. Crane [24] and exemplified, to select a notable example to which I have already alluded, in M. H. Abrams' account of the structure and genesis of the greater Romantic lyric.[25] Through such study we could come to a fuller and more accurate understanding of literature as a primary manifestation of the characteristic freedom of the human spirit, its capacity to invent and develop *in* time forms of imaginative self-discovery and expression which in their aesthetic autonomy are a chief vehicle of its triumph *over* time.

[24] See Crane's "Critical and Historical Principles of Literary History," in *The Idea of the Humanities and Other Essays Critical and Historical* (Chicago, 1967), I, 45–156; reprinted separately as a paperback with a foreword by Sheldon Sacks.

[25] "Structure and Style in the Greater Romantic Lyric," in *From Sensibility to Romanticism: Essays Presented to Frederick A. Pottle*, ed. Harold Bloom and Frederick W. Hilles (New York, 1965), pp. 527–60.

IRVIN EHRENPREIS

Meaning:

IMPLICIT AND EXPLICIT

MAYNARD MACK has suggested that Mark Van Doren probably started the vogue of the phrase "poetry of statement." [1] Van Doren applied the phrase to Dryden's genius: "His poetry was the poetry of statement. At his best he wrote without figures, without transforming passion. . . ." [2] Reviewing Van Doren's book, T. S. Eliot said, "Dryden's words . . . are precise, they state immensely, but their suggestiveness is often nothing." [3] The phrase "poetry of statement" and its associations soon attached themselves to the poetry of Pope, but they recall Johnson's description of Swift's work: "He pays no court to the passions; he excites neither surprise nor admiration; he always understands himself and his reader always understands him." [4]

[1] "Wit and Poetry and Pope," n. 1, in *Pope and His Contemporaries: Essays Presented to George Sherburn* (Oxford, 1949), p. 20.
[2] *The Poetry of John Dryden* (New York, 1926), Ch. 3, par. 2.
[3] "John Dryden," last par.   [4] *Swift*, par. 113.

We can stop now and agree that these critics share the impression that they have missed nothing important in the meaning of the writers they are judging; and I think no eminent critic, unless he has made a special study of the century following the Restoration, feels otherwise. I am sure they are wrong, but their impression reflects what I believe is a genuine part of the characteristic work of that century, a faith in explicit meaning. It is because the so-called Augustans—if I may stretch the term to include the chief figures in English literature from 1660 to 1760—it is because the Augustans seldom trust connotation, emblem, image, or allegory alone, to convey their meaning—because they normally make explicit any doctrine they wish to inculcate, that the older critics could so easily ignore other features of their work. Even those brilliant compositions that embody dangerous doctrines in politics and religion, or particular satires on eminent men, will usually be found to include explicit, discursive passages to orientate the reader and keep him from misunderstanding the argument.

It is also a feature of this literature that the author conceives of himself as illustrating or enhancing his explicit meaning through the resources of his art—through similes, splendid language, expressive versification. In fact, this feature is an inevitable consequence of the desire for clarity, because such a desire implies that the same doctrine can be expressed either clearly or obscurely without essentially changing as doctrine—in other words, that the same meaning can be conveyed in different styles. Dryden in his translation of Virgil's *Georgics* says,

> Nor can I doubt what oil I must bestow,
> To raise my subject from a ground so low:
> And the mean matter which my theme affords,
> T'embellish with magnificence of words. (III. 453–56)

The conception of style as the frame of meaning, or (even worse) as ornament applied to meaning, is as monstrous a crime as exists in the jurisprudence of modern criticism. We pledge our allegiance to a principle of organic form that makes style and meaning indivisible. As used by many critics in the last forty years, this principle no longer means a harmony of conception that allows for great freedom and variety of expression. It has come to imply that the deep or true structure of a work of art need not appear on its surface, that a poem which at first hearing sounds disjointed or incoherent may possess an inner shape disclosed by patterns of imagery or other elements that are not expository or discursive. If a scholar is handling a poem written before the doctrine of organic form was widely accepted, and he nevertheless wishes to demonstrate that this poem exemplifies the principle of organic form quite as well as Romantic and Symbolist poems, his most dazzling feat will be to reveal in it a structure that seems independent of the explicit meaning or that at points even contradicts it. "Structure" in such an operation comes to denote something at odds with the old idea of a rhetorical skeleton or a narrative plot. Yet this crypto-schema may be as rigid as the genres and patterns from which it was supposed to free us.

In keeping with the supposed principle of organic form some modern scholars give their best energy to the labor of drawing meaning out of what Dryden would have considered the secondary elements of an Augustan poem, viz., the connotations of words, figures, images, allusions. In so doing, the scholars naturally give small attention to the explicit passages, except to suggest that those are less explicit than they sound. In other words, they tend to strip the explicit passages of the very attribute of meaning which they then bestow on the other ingredients of the poem. In their eagerness to show that the concep-

tion of style as frame or ornament cannot account for the design
of Augustan masterpieces, a few interpreters make it appear that
explicit meaning is not even a fundamental part of the poet's
design. The frame thus replaces the picture.

Another characteristic of Augustan poetry also troubles us.
Not only has the meaning of such poetry seemed clear. It has
often seemed unexciting as well. Satire attacking men in high
places may be bold and dangerous. But the moral doctrines on
which Augustan satire rests are usually commonplace. Yet the
modern critic, especially since the Second World War, has sin-
gled out for praise the kind of doctrine that is either subversive
of received opinions or profoundly original. It is hard to praise
the explicit doctrine of Augustan poems for boldness, originality, or subtlety, when the poet claims in his work to be teaching
familiar doctrines and to be making them fresh through his presentation.

What one finds therefore in many re-interpretations of Augustan literature is a flight from explicit meaning. At its least adven-
turous and most persuasive this flight represents a desire to
enlarge a literary work, to give it a moral or intellectual setting,
that must enrich its suggestiveness and make it appear not so
different after all from the haunting, evocative literature to
which it was opposed by critics like Van Doren, Eliot, and
Tillyard.

When the critic merely provides a moral or intellectual setting, he may recognize a poem's explicit meaning. But he tries to
show that while this may seem declarative and commonplace, it
is in fact alive with connotation. He does so by connecting the
work with traditions that modern readers have lost sight of.
What seems shallow today, says the scholar, had rich reverbera-
tions in its own time. So he demonstrates that the theme of a

poem evokes intellectual principles and moral ideas long and widely held by a great line of poets, philosophers, theologians. Among such doctrines or themes are the chain of being, the value of the contemplative life, concordia discors, the golden mean. Sometimes they are tied together with a religious motif like the doctrine of atonement. One wonders where students of seventeenth-century poetry would be without the Fall of Man, a doctrine better known to students of the novel as the Rise of the Middle Class.

I should like to make some distinctions here. One is between the origin of a poem and its meaning. It is a valuable and fascinating job of research to discover what forces worked upon the imagination of a genius while he was creating a great poem. But such biographical and genetic studies do not reveal the depth or the meaning of the poem unless the poem invites us to think of them. Even if the poem does in itself evoke ancient traditions, while those may indeed give the lines resonance, they cannot by that effect make the meaning either profound or daring unless the doctrines are in fact profound or daring, at least to the living reader. No amount of resonance can give sonority to the Golden Mean. The scholar who validates the argument of a poem by showing that its doctrines were widely accepted by a long line of deep thinkers puts himself in an awkward position if those doctrines seem shallow. He is implicitly saying they are not shallow but commonplace.

In his studies of Pope's poetry, Maynard Mack sometimes implies that he is enhancing the literary value of a work when he is in a most rewarding way disclosing its origins. Professor Mack observes that Pope in a few lines of one poem echoes Cowley's paraphrase of a famous passage from Virgil's *Georgics*, celebrating the farmer's life:

Court-virtues bear, like gems, the highest rate,
Born where Heav'n's influence scarce can penetrate:
In life's low vale, the soil the virtues like,
They please as beauties, here as wonders strike.

                              (Pope, *Epistle to Cobham*, ll. 93–96)

If this does echo Cowley, we are told, "the Virgilian passage
masses behind Pope's contrast of court and country the most authoritative of all literary precedents." [5]

Now I am puzzled what to make of this. The lines in Pope's
poem are deeply ironical and framed in a conceit of Pope's own
elaboration. Nothing in the lines invites us to look for literary
allusions. Professor Mack carefully observes that Pope is not deliberately alluding to Virgil or Cowley. Such a passage, he says,
shows "at the most reminiscence, not allusion" (p. 85). But the
fact is that the passage is less enriched than confused if one
brings in Virgil. Pope here is opposing the difficulty of being
virtuous at court to the ease of being virtuous in an obscure life;
he does not contrast city and country. Virgil compares the serenity of the philosopher with that of the farmer, and says his
own first wish is to understand astronomy and other natural
sciences; but if he cannot do so much, he would like to live a
country life. It is true, as Victorian editors pointed out, that
Pope probably echoes Cowley here. But as it happens, he may

[5] *The Garden and the City* (Toronto, 1969), p. 83. The line by Cowley
(Essay No. 4, "Of Agriculture," the translation "out of Virgil," l. 47)
which Pope echoes does not in fact belong to Virgil's praise of the
farmer's life as such (*Georgics* II. 458–74) but to a neighboring passage.
Any reader making Professor Mack's connection, therefore, would have
to identify Pope's line as taken from Cowley's and then would have to
move back from the corresponding line in Virgil (*Georgics* II. 485) to the
earlier lines.

also be echoing a passage from a comedy by Dryden, in which the hero operatically prefers courts to cottages (*Marriage-à-la-Mode*, II.i.439–47). It seems to me that the more specifically we recall the antecedents of Pope's lines, the more remote the intrinsic, witty art of those lines becomes. Of course, we do have to keep in mind a vague tradition of opposing rural retirement to courtly ambition; yet the lines themselves evoke that. It is always fascinating to learn that Pope may have based his own poetry on that of others; but if allusions and echoes do not seem deliberately employed in a poem, they can hardly be said to enrich its meaning. I wonder what we gain by diverting a reader from the text to a reminiscence. After all, one never knows how many echoes one has failed to hear.

In another subtle and learned argument Professor Mack declares that toward the end of Pope's *Epistle to Bathurst* the author deliberately alludes to an ode of Horace. To put the case briefly, we are told first that Pope's poem shows so many clusters of thematic parallels to Horace's ode that anyone familiar with the Latin lines would think of them when he reads the English. Within this context we are invited to read a couplet from the *Epistle* as a witty allusion to the myth of Danaë:

'Till all the Dæmon makes his full descent
In one abundant show'r of cent. per cent.
                                          (*To Bathurst*, ll. 371–72)

Since the ode by Horace opens with a peculiar interpretation of the myth, and since Pope implies the same interpretation, Professor Mack concludes that the English poet here "directs our attention squarely" to the Latin ode (Mack, p. 88).

I wonder how demonstrative such reasoning is. The themes

common to Horace's ode and Pope's epistle also pervade the satires of Persius, Nos., III, V, and VI [6] (not to mention other works
that deal with the power of gold); and Persius was a favorite of
Pope's. [7] The couplet that reminds some scholars of Jove's descent on Danaë might remind others of Apollo's descent on the
sibyl in the *Aeneid*. [8] Even if one agreed that this couplet alludes
to the myth of Danaë, it so happens that precisely the version of
the myth used by Horace appears in an epigram of Paulus Silentiarius (*Greek Anthology* v.217), a poet whom Pope echoed
elsewhere (*Rape of the Lock*, II.23–28). [9] I doubt that even Dr.

[6] See especially Dryden's translation, for language anticipating that
of Pope's epistle. In Satire III the anecdote of the sick man is used much
as Pope uses the fable of Balaam.

[7] Austin Warren, *Alexander Pope as Critic and Humanist* (Princeton,
1929), p. 200; Pope, *Correspondence*, ed. G. Sherburn (Oxford, 1956), I,
99 and II, 231.

[8] Compare the language of Dryden's *Aeneid* VI.78–87, 120–25 with
that of Pope's *Bathurst*, ll. 371–74. (Dryden's l. 117—between the passages I indicate—is echoed by Pope in *Bathurst*, ll. 75–77.) Or else,
combining the idea of rain with sexual possession, and anticipating
Pope's language, there is Dryden's translation of Virgil *Georgics*
II.440–41: "For then almighty Jove descends, and pours / Into his
buxom bride his fruitful show'rs." For other anticipations of Pope's language by Dryden, see the translations of Virgil *Pastorals* VII.83: "Jove
descends in show'rs of kindly rain"; Persius I. 91; and Ovid *Elegies*
II.xix; also *Annus Mirabilis*, l. 52. It may be worth observing that Reuben Brower, in a peculiarly "Horatian" study of the *Epistle to Bathurst*,
failed to hear any echo of Horace in ll. 371–74; see his *Alexander Pope:
The Poetry of Allusion* (Oxford, 1959), pp. 251–60 and passim.

[9] In connection with the myth of Danaë, the very expression that
Professor Mack finds so significant in Horace, viz., "*converto in pretium
deo*," is used (in Greek) not only by Paulus Silentiarius but also by other
poets of the Greek Anthology: Antipater (v.31.5) and Bassus
(v.125.1). Cf. also Parmenion (v.33 and 34), Asclepiades (v.64.6), Pal-
ladas (v.257.2), and Strabo (v.239.2).

Bentley, when he saw Pope's line "In one abundant show'r of cent. per cent." murmured to himself the opening stanza of Horace's ode.[10]

The section of the *Epistle to Bathurst* to which the couplet in question belongs is the tale of Sir Balaam. This is a heavy-handed fable preaching the hollowest morality. Its obvious meaning is that people who by evil devices get rich quickly will come to a bad end. I'm not sure how this doctrine would be enhanced by an allusion to Horace's ode, in which the poet says he lengthens his purse by contracting his desires. But even with Horace's support the doctrine would remain hollow. Allusion as such may decorate; it cannot deepen.[11]

General allusions, or allusions to context offer a wider escape route from explicit meaning than one gains through particular allusions. In these analyses the critic assumes that when a poet does echo a line or passage from an earlier work by another poet, the reader ought to recall the whole of that earlier work and ought to use it as enlarging the significance of the poem at hand. The first question here is whether in any case there is such a general allusion. Scholars have a cheerful way of assuming there is none when the earlier work would not fit their scheme of interpretation. If Pope in *The Rape of the Lock* echoes MacSwiney's *Camilla*, most scholars are content to identify the indebtedness and say no more. But if Pope echoes *Paradise Lost*, they bring to bear a whole system of Protestant theology in order to explicate the Roman Catholic's poem.

[10] In his extensive notes to *Bathurst*, Pope draws our attention to echoes of Virgil (ll. 75, 184) and Juvenal (l. 394—copied by Johnson in *London*). If he had wished us to hear an echo of Horace in ll. 371–72, he could surely have provided a note as a pointer.

[11] I am using "decorate" in a favorable sense, as, for example, making a doctrine seductive. I am using "deepen" only in relation to meaning or doctrine.

Earl Wasserman suggests that in the *Rape of the Lock*, when the heroine dreams of her guardian sylph Ariel, the poem invites us to think of *Paradise Lost* and of Satan tempting Eve.[12] If the poem does so, I should say it is by the subtlest of hints. But Ariel's speech clearly echoes the *Aeneid*, Psalm xci, and various poems by Dryden, as one may see from the notes to Tillotson's edition. It is clear as well that the important echoes of *Paradise Lost* are from the speeches of the angels, Gabriel and Uriel, in Book IV, figures naturally associated with Ariel because they guard Eve as he guards Belinda. It is further clear that of all the echoes those of the *Aeneid* dominate the passage. If a scholar wishes to make Ariel's character satanic, in contradiction to all these signs and to the tone of the passage in Pope's poem, I cannot disprove his interpretation. But I can marvel at those who accept it.

I should like to call attention to one feature of Pope's work that may throw light on his allusiveness, although this feature is external to the poetry. In a few places Pope uses a footnote to direct the reader's ear to a literary echo. It has been argued that the notes are a sign that Pope expected all such echoes, noted or not, to be observed.[13] But is this logical? Precisely the opposite seems to me the case. If Pope thought he could rely on the reader to recognize the echoes, he would supply no notes at all for the purpose. At one point he identifies a striking allusion to the opening line of the fourth Book of the *Aeneid*—this was by far the best known book of the best known of all poems, and Pope felt he had to identify the allusion (*Rape of the Lock*, IV.1). The existence of such notes suggests to me that the poet had a

[12] Earl Wasserman, "The Limits of Allusion in *The Rape of the Lock*," *JEGP*, 65 (1966), 425–44.
[13] Wasserman, par. 3.

proper opinion of the illiteracy of his readers. After all, Montaigne had to read his adored Plutarch in French.[14]

Since so many authors and works are echoed in *The Rape of the Lock*, it becomes a subtle exercise to determine which of them, at many points, the poem may be reflecting. But it is still worth observing that at least three eighteenth-century critics—Dennis, Johnson, and Warton—considered the relation of the poem to its predecessors without observing any Virgilian or Miltonic parodies that Pope himself failed to annotate; and yet they did discuss the parallels with Boileau which Pope ignores. Dennis's *Remarks on the Rape of the Lock* are little more than a running comparison of Pope's masterpiece with Boileau's *Lutrin*. One might ask whether the deficiency of these critics lay in their knowledge of Latin or of English.[15]

Even when a poet boldly alludes to another man's work and draws our attention to the fact, the significance of the parallel depends on how he applies it. We have no way of telling whether or not the poet asks us to recall the whole of the work he alludes to; we have no way of telling whether he supports or condemns the meaning of that work, except from the use of the

[14] For additional evidence supporting this position, see Dryden's references to Virgil in the notes to *Annus Mirabilis*, Swift's references to Homer in the notes to *The Battle of the Books*, and Pope's notes on his imitations in *The Dunciad*. The references of Dryden and Pope to Book One of the *Aeneid* will startle anybody who admires the literacy of Augustan readers.

[15] See the following: John Dennis, *Critical Works*, ed. E. N. Hooker (Baltimore, Md., 1939–43), II, 329, 341–42 and passim; Johnson, *Pope*, pars. 53–60, 335–41; Joseph Warton, *An Essay on the Genius and Writings of Pope* (2 vols., 1756, 1782), passim; Alexander F. B. Clark, *Boileau and French Classical Criticism in England (1660–1830)* (Paris, 1925), p. 10 and passim.

allusion in his own poem. Allusions are dumb witnesses until they are cross-examined.

For example, Professor Wasserman comments on an echo of Psalm xci in *The Rape of the Lock* and assumes that the poet intends it ironically, viz., that the satanic Ariel is ruining Belinda through the very language in which the Psalmist promises that God will protect the faithful (Wasserman, par. 11). We are directed as well to another couplet describing Belinda in words that recall Virgil's description of Dido when the queen burns with secret love for Aeneas. Here we are asked to find a true parallel, and to read the poem as implying that Belinda, for all her coquetry, really desires to be loved just as Dido did.[16]

But supposing we admit that these two echoes are deliberate allusions to context—if we then wish to decide that one is ironical and the other straightforward, we must read Pope's poem. When we do so, I think it will appear that the first echo is used simply and the second ironically. From the language and tone in which the poet explicitly and consistently describes the sylph, it is more probable that Ariel's character is benignly similar to that of Uriel and Gabriel than that it is devilishly opposed to theirs; in the words of the Psalmist, Ariel will defend Belinda against the dangers of night and of day. As for the echo of Virgil's description of Dido, it is not through this that we discover Belinda's wish to be loved. On the contrary, it is through the explicit words of Pope in the preceding canto, when he declares that an earthly lover lurks at her heart (*Rape* III.144). So there is nothing to be revealed in that region of her character. Describing Belinda as Dido, Pope says that "anxious cares the pensive

---

[16] Wasserman, "The Limits of Allusion," par. 17; *Rape* IV.1; *Aeneid* IV. 1. The identity of the line references in the *Rape* and the *Aeneid* is hardly accidental, and it would have made Pope's note quite unnecessary if he had supposed he could trust the reader's memory of Virgil.

nymph opprest, / And secret passions labour'd in her breast"; a few lines below, he explicitly enumerates the passions as "rage, resentment and despair," surely an ironical contrast to the amorous fire consuming Dido (*Rape* IV.1–2, 9).

My attitude may be mistaken, and the art of *The Rape of the Lock* may indeed depend on the sort of reader who could treat all the parallels given in Tillotson's notes as general allusions. But whoever wishes to convert me to that view had better not start by declaring that Ariel is satanic, that Belinda is criminal, and that Clarissa, who hands the Baron the scissors when he wishes to cut the lock, is the character to whom we must look for moral enlightenment.[17] As for those who imagine that Pope systematically condemns Belinda's society for failing to meet the heroic standards of Achilles and Hector, they might do worse than to read Pope's translation of the *Iliad* and observe how deeply he is embarrassed by the coarseness, the cruelty, the boastfulness, and mendacity of Homer's heroes; and they might consider how much Pope perhaps thought Agamemnon could learn from the higher civilization of England under Queen Anne.

The analysis of general allusions sometimes broadens to the point where works by two authors are set side by side as if the earlier were a consistently revealing parallel to the later. Here the scholar sometimes assumes that the model or source (if it is one) has fundamental meanings which are preserved (either simply or ironically) in the later work. An age of mock-epics, mock-pastorals, and free translations seems peculiarly suited to this approach. If Fielding uses the *Aeneid* as the general pattern for his novel *Amelia*, it seems fair to suspect that the role of Miss Matthews, who seduces the hero while they are both in the same jail, has moral implications like those which Virgil drew

[17] I do not mean that Pope disagrees with Clarissa's advice, but that he treats it here as a decorative formula.

from Dido's seduction of Aeneas. But we can make the inference with confidence because Fielding explicitly passes on Captain Booth the same judgment that Mercury delivers to Aeneas.

When there is no explicit statement, our doubts cannot be easily resolved. A writer may use an earlier work as his pattern without adopting its implications. Swift, in *The Battle of the Books*, bases the action generally on that of the *Aeneid* and the *Iliad*. So he describes Wotton planning to kill Sir William Temple and echoes Virgil's description of Arruns planning to kill the female warrior Camilla. It is conceivable that some scholar might therefore identify Temple with Camilla and argue that Swift was making a comment on his patron's masculinity. Nobody could disprove such an argument, and I dare not estimate how many would be persuaded by it.

Martin Price has tried to account for Dryden's *Absalom and Achitophel* largely in terms of *Paradise Lost*.[18] This interpretation

[18] Martin Price, *To the Palace of Wisdom* (New York, 1964), pp. 52–62. This line of interpretation goes back to A. W. Verrall, who called attention to Dryden's echoes of Milton and suggested that *Absalom and Achitophel* might be a miniature epic with satirical elements (*Lectures on Dryden*, ed. Margaret Verrall [Cambridge, 1914], p. 59 and passim). See also the following: Van Doren, (cited in n. 2 above), who says it was almost exclusively the diction of Milton—rather than anything else in his poetry—that influenced Dryden (end of Ch. 3); E. M. W. Tillyard, *Poetry Direct and Oblique* (1934), pp. 81–88; Bonamy Dobrée, "Milton and Dryden: A Comparison in Poetic Ideas and Poetic Method," *ELH*, 13 (1936), 83–100; Ruth Wallerstein, "To Madness Near Allied: Shaftesbury and His Place in *Absalom and Achitophel*," *HLQ*, 6 (1943), 445–71 (and the perceptive review by H. Trowbridge, *PQ*, 23 [1944], 164); Ian Jack, *Augustan Satire: Intention and Idiom in English Poetry*, 1660–1750 (Oxford, 1952), pp. 61–62 and n. 6 (replying acutely to Verrall); Morris Freedman, "Dryden's Miniature Epic," *JEGP*, 57 (1958), 211–19; Bernard Schilling, *Dryden and the Conservative Myth: A Reading of Absalom and Achitophel* (New Haven, 1961), pp. 136–37 and passim; Anne Da-

he frames in a scheme of moral principles derived from Pascal and Blake. So we are asked to understand the meaning of Dryden's poem not only in the language of Milton's but also in the categories of "energy," "order of the flesh," "order of the mind," and "order of the spirit." Now it happens that Dryden includes in *Absalom and Achitophel* a long passage of fifty-nine lines (752–810) clearly expounding the doctrine of his poem. This quite explicit passage Professor Price touches on in a few misleading sentences (p. 62); but to Dryden's supposed parallels with Milton he devotes paragraphs of analysis. His effort leads to surprising outcomes.

When Dryden calls the restive English people in 1681 "Adam-wits" (l. 51), we are asked to see a contrast with Milton's view of Adam as a man of "intuitive wisdom" (Price, p. 54). But Dryden is suggesting a parallel with Adam, not a contrast; and he does not allude to wisdom as such. He is saying that, like Adam, many Englishmen do not appreciate true liberty when they possess it: in his words, they are "too fortunately free" (l. 51). Dryden's view is anti-Puritan. He is describing the Whigs here as rebellious Puritans, impatient of constitutional monarchy and demanding a republic. Later, in the passage of exposition, he makes the same point, in case we have failed to grasp it earlier (ll. 755–56). Precisely the rebelliousness that Milton would approve, Dryden naturally condemns.

Professor Price finds that Dryden relates Absalom's lawless self-indulgence to David's sexual promiscuity, and we are asked to treat "energy" as a category that includes both impulses. We are then to connect the unruliness of the people with the idea of

---

vidson Ferry, *Milton and the Miltonic Dryden* (Cambridge, Mass., 1968), passim; Leonora Brodwin, "Miltonic Allusion in *Absalom and Achitophel*: Its Function in the Political Satire," *JEGP*, 58 (1969), 24–44.

energy and with sexual excess. But in fact Dryden attributes a
rebellious nature to characters who are abstemious and who lack
sexuality. The poet in *Absalom and Achitophel* never suggests that
Absalom's depravity is related to his father's sexual habits, and
the poem never links the unruliness of the people with either a
general concept of energy or the king's promiscuity.

A Puritan might indeed do so; and Milton in *Paradise Lost* says
that men, by letting their passions subdue their reason, make
themselves fit to be ruled by political tyrants, or kings
(xi.90–101). But Dryden, as Professor Price observes, contrasts
the free sexuality of King Charles with the abstinence of his
enemy Lord Shaftesbury; for his lordship punishes "a body
which he . . . coud not please" (l. 167) and in place of many
children begets one unpromising son. The poet associates
Shaftesbury and his followers with Puritan "zeal" (l. 181) and
with republican government (ll. 226–27). The poet says explicitly that the people's rebelliousness was innate (ll. 214–19) and
not due to the king's character.

Other scholars have gone even further in founding an interpretation of *Absalom and Achitophel* upon Milton's works. One
writes as though Dryden must have learned common Biblical
expressions like "sons of Belial" from *Paradise Lost*, although the
two poets give those words different implications.[19] Those who
follow such lines notice too lightly that each poet made the Bible
and the *Aeneid* the main source of his greatest poem. The "Miltonic" scholars underweight the fact that the story of David,
Absalom, and Achitophel was repeatedly applied to kings in
general and to Charles II in particular before Dryden wrote his

[19] Ferry (cited in preceding note), p. 31; cf. James Kinsley's note on
l. 598 of *Absalom and Achitophel* in his edition of Dryden's *Poems* (Oxford, 1958), IV, 1892.

satire.[20] They seldom observe that the satanism of Achitophel and the parallel with the Fall of Man were part of the tradition Dryden received. One sometimes gets the impression that when Moses wrote the Pentateuch, he was inspired less by Jehovah than by Milton, and that the structure of the *Aeneid* is derived from that of *Paradise Lost*.

Parallels with *Paradise Lost* teach one little about the meaning of *Absalom and Achitophel*. Dryden at points may describe Achitophel in terms derived from Milton. But the great confrontation between Achitophel and Absalom recalls *Paradise Regained*, which Professor Price does not mention, as well as *Paradise Lost*. To press the parallels farther than a similarity of action and rhetoric seems dangerous. It is one thing to regard Achitophel as satanic. Dryden in the poem explicitly describes him as false, cursed, secretive, crooked, ambitious, "implacable in hate," and so forth. We don't have to read *Paradise Lost* to connect the devil with Achitophel. But when Absalom is tempted by him, should we think of Eve? of Christ? of the fallen angels seduced by Lucifer? of all these?

Is it not a rash enterprise to hunt in a poem which attacks Puritan principles and exalts Charles II, for the teachings of a poem that attacks monarchists as diabolical and exalts Puritan principles? If one had to set *Absalom and Achitophel* beside *Paradise Lost*, surely the correlation would be inverse. Where Dryden gives divine sanction to Charles II but identifies the wicked Achitophel with democracy and rebellion, Milton describes all

[20] See Hugh Macdonald, *John Dryden: A Bibliography of Early Editions and of Drydeniana* (Oxford, 1939), pp. 18–19; Howard Schless, "Dryden's *Absalom and Achitophel* and *A Dialogue between Nathan and Absolome*," PQ, 40 (1961), 139–43; John M. Wallace, "Dryden and History: A Problem in Allegorical Reading," *ELH*, 36 (1969), 280–81.

kings as rebels against divine authority (XII.24–37). One might perhaps read *Absalom and Achitophel* as a reply to *Paradise Lost*. It seems Quixotic to read it as an echo.[21]

The action of Dryden's poem is indeed designed to follow that of another poem, but that other poem is neither *Paradise Lost* nor *Paradise Regained*. It is the Second Book of Samuel, Chapters thirteen to nineteen. On the Biblical story Dryden founds an allegory of the history of Charles II, his son the Duke of Monmouth, and the Whig leader the Earl of Shaftesbury. Into this story Dryden may perhaps incorporate large parallels with *Paradise Lost* and *Paradise Regained;* he certainly alludes to the Second Book of Samuel in general and to half a dozen other books of the Bible, to say nothing of the *Aeneid* and Ovid's *Metamorphoses*. To single out *Paradise Lost* from this complex and to make it the highway into Dryden's argument seems a flight from explicit meaning.

The broadest and most evocative parallel with another literary work is still less liberating than the removal of a poem from one great moral tradition to another, the discovery, for example, that *The Rape of the Lock*, so far from sympathizing with the society it represents, really condemns it. When a scholar puts aside the questions of source, influence, or allusion, and simply reclassifies a work as belonging to an order of works and doctrines it has never been pictured with, one sees shutters opening and one gasps at vistas of forbidden landscapes. Generally, a scholar uses this route in order to arrive at a subversive meaning for a poem that had seemed orthodox. But the purpose may also be to reduce an apparently iconoclastic poem to orthodox morality.

[21] Leonora Brodwin (cited in n. 18 above) has interpreted *Absalom and Achitophel* as a tissue of ironical allusions to Milton's works. According to her, the poem requires the reader not only to recognize the allusions but to understand that they are generally unsympathetic to Milton.

When the explicit meaning militates against new interpretations, we have the interesting case of a work that seems openly daring but that is—or so the critic says—insidiously conventional.

I must again make some distinctions. In examining the meaning of a poem, one finds some opinions or generalizations that seem particularly to be enforced by the argument, structure, and connotations. These I call the doctrine. There are others which appear as commonplaces with which nobody could disagree. They are taken for granted as casual opinion, neither recommended nor attacked. These I call formulae.

The more commonplace a principle is, the more emphatic an author has to be if he wishes to make a point of teaching it—of presenting it as doctrine rather than assuming it as formula. A contempt for the mob of common people, an admiration for the English political constitution, when casually expressed, cannot be significant. It must be a formula. If a writer takes a principle for granted in his work, the alert reader will assume little from it about the meaning of the work. This is particularly so in the period 1660–1760, when doctrines that are not blasphemous or politically subversive are normally expounded as well as illustrated. In a dramatic work this is supremely true, because unless the doctrine is explicitly conveyed by a sympathetic character, we have no way of telling whether it is a commonplace formula or a part of some characterization or a genuine doctrine advocated by the author.

Now no religious principle is more commonplace, more widely accepted—by ancient Greeks, by Mohammedans, and by Christians—than that of divine Providence, the principle that the gods intervene in human life so as to assist the virtuous and to frustrate the wicked. In the finest comedies of the Restoration period few readers have found this doctrine expounded or illustrated, because the amoral character of the protagonists is so striking. From Dorimant in *The Man of Mode* to Mirabell in *The Way of the World* the man on whom fortune smiles lacks the marks of Christian goodness.

Aubrey Williams has recently decided that this view is wrong; and he has argued that in fact the plays of Congreve are "brilliant demonstrations of a providential order in human event that is fully analogous to the greater world of providential order insisted upon not only by contemporary Anglican theologians but also insisted upon by contemporary literary critics as a fundamental dramatic principle. . . . the works of Congreve are fully conformable to the Christian vision of human experience which still prevailed at the end of the 17th century. . . ." [22]

This lively departure from received opinion is supported by analyses of the structure and the language of the plays. We are told that through complicated plots that fit the descriptions given by literary critics and by priests of the workings of Providential justice, Congreve dramatizes the Christian idea.

I myself would think twice before identifying as a Christian principle a belief that God intervenes on the side of virtue. As a religious institution Christianity has never lacked presumption. But we need not add to the wealth of so prosperous a corporation this commonest of properties. Complicated plots in which the schemes of villains are defeated by sympathetic characters through the operation of surprising coincidences are the mainstay of comedy from Menander to Molière. It would be a delicate job of carpentry to join the use of such plots to any single moral philosophy or religious doctrine. My comments will be limited to two of the examples offered.

Love for Love is a play that gives much attention to supernatural interventions in human affairs. The reason is the same as in

[22] Aubrey Williams, "Poetical Justice, the Contrivances of Providence, and the Works of William Congreve," *ELH*, 35 (1968), p. 541.

its ancestor, Dryden's *Evening's Love*, viz., that one of the comic butts is a silly astrologer—here named Foresight. Professor Williams says *Love for Love* is "saturated with Christian imagery and diction," and that there is no evidence for calling its perspective "naturalistic" (p. 559). But he spreads out the net of Christian language until it holds the many references to prophecies that are or are not fulfilled in connection with Foresight's obsession, and he also includes quasi-religious expressions that belong to common speech. Would it be unkind to observe that in this sense *The Land of Heart's Desire* and *Sunday Morning* are saturated with Christian imagery and diction? Nowhere in *Love for Love* is the doctrine of a providential order explicitly discussed, as it is in Dryden's dedication of his *Aeneid* and in Johnson's *Irene*. Congreve's references to Providence—if they are such—remain casual and formulaic.

To describe sexual passion in the language of religious devotion is an old habit of the poets, and has been considered blasphemous by some pious critics. One recalls Harriet, at the end of *The Man of Mode*, condemning Loveit for making a god of Dorimant. So Congreve can hardly appear eccentric if he has the characters in *Love for Love* follow this practice. The profusion of such language near the beginning and end of the play suggests that the author draws the usual comic parallel between the attitude of lovers toward courtship and that of religious persons toward worship. When Valentine (who regrets that the baby farmer looking after one of his bastards has not smothered it) finally secures the heroine to be his bride, he says to one of his rivals, "You would have interposed between me and Heav'n; but Providence laid Purgatory [i.e., marriage, by trickery, to a promiscuous woman] in your way—You have but justice" (v,i.595–97). Professor Williams takes this remark as an indication of Congreve's theology, and asks, "How much more explicit

can a playwright possibly be about the Providential relevance of
the poetical justice he has exemplified in a play?" (p.560) One
hesitates to reply, the choice is so varied. But surely we are not
to suppose that Congreve believed in Purgatory!

When a scholar describes Valentine, the hero of *Love for Love*
as "exemplifying the traditional Christian paradox that one kind
of madness occasionally to be found in this world may be in the
eyes of Heaven, the highest kind of wisdom" (pp.559–60), he
perhaps demonstrates the happy elasticity of the word "Christian." Boccaccio's story of the lover who sacrificed his favorite
falcon in order to feast his beloved—a woman on whom he had
squandered his wealth—seems more illuminating than such a
view.[23] Valentine, who has wasted his fortune in pleasure for
the sake of Angelica, pretends insanity to avoid being disin-
herited and to persuade Angelica to confess that she loves him.
When his scheme fails and he believes Angelica will marry his
own father, he agrees in despair to give up his claim to the estate. She is then so deeply touched by his fidelity that she does
declare her love.

Professor Williams contrasts Valentine with the other characters, who "seek their own most selfish purposes" while the hero
is "willing to be mad enough to ruin himself for love of another"
(pp. 559–60). But alas the selfishness of the other characters—such as it is—consists largely in their wishing to enjoy the
sexual pleasures that Valentine has been enjoying and to marry
a fortune as Valentine wishes to do. In the matter of deceit only
an expert casuist could settle the precedence between Valentine
and his rivals. Professor Williams finds Congreve's plays Providential in design because he concentrates on the character of the

[23] *Decameron*, Fifth Day, Ninth Story. For this suggestion I am indebted to Maximillian Novak, *William Congreve* (New York, 1971), p.
108.

villains. Those who examine the heroes will find them pagan.

As Professor Williams observes, Congreve makes no explicit reference to Providence as such in *The Way of the World*. Yet we are asked to see in the magnificent complexity of the plot and the happy resolution of Marwood's devilish schemes, Congreve's "most polished justification of the contrivances of Providence" (p. 562). For an illustrative parallel we are referred to lines from the *Essay on Man* (II.175). To which I reply, precisely: Pope explicitly argues in support of the doctrine; and because it is so commonplace, he argues with great emphasis and clarity. Congreve does not.

It is confusing to be told that some works must teach Christian Providential doctrine because they explicitly argue for it, while other works must do so because they exemplify it with no overt declaration. In fact, however, even if an epilogue appeared at the end of *The Way of the World* to say that the play was demonstration of divine Providence, I would dismiss the declaration as a formula. In the character of Mirabell what is there to deserve divine intervention? the fact that when he thought his cast-off mistress was pregnant, he married her to an old friend? Just how does Mirabell exemplify faith, hope, and charity? It is surely because the evil of characters like Marwood is matched by no saintly goodness on the other side that the plays cannot embody any transcendent moral doctrine.

Such interpretations derive from the insistence that all the elements of a poem must cohere, that no part can be without meaning, that no digression may serve as mere decorative entertainment. Each element must be significant in its own right, and its significance must have an important relation to that of all the others. Every subplot must somehow reflect the main plot. Every striking effect of versification must be parallel to a striking sense. The design of the action cannot be pleasingly symmetrical; its symmetry must suggest a divine symmetry, or else it must be ironically contrasted with social chaos. This is a false idea of organic form, which properly refers to a harmony of conception, allowing for great freedom and variety in expression.

When the critic tries to apply false notions of coherence to a poem, he sometimes finds no allusions or parallels that will integrate a stubborn passage into his scheme. If he cannot let the passage stand as diverting ornament or as one of many possible developments of the original conception, if he holds it firmly in his scheme and demands that it yield up an appropriate meaning, he may at last choose the literary equivalent of *mettre à la question*, and that is an interpretation through allegory. Now it is unlikely that an Augustan poet would erect an allegory in a poem without warning the reader, unless the meaning were blasphemous, immoral, or politically subversive. When Dryden wrote *The Hind and the Panther*, he rendered the genre and the argument of his poem perhaps too clear.

But Brendan O Hehir has taken another approach to *Coopers Hill*, Denham's long poem which deals with a series of prospects or views to be seen from a hill near Windsor, and with the associations—historical and political—of those prospects.[24] As Denham in the poem thinks of various moral and political doctrines, he discusses them explicitly until two-thirds of the way through, when he describes a stag hunt that occupies most of the remainder (ll. 241–322 out of 358 lines in the poem). The hunt could easily suggest to the reader several Aesopian fables in which a stag figures;[25] and in one couplet the fleeing stag is

[24] Brendan O Hehir, *Expans'd Hieroglyphicks: A Study of Sir John Denham's Coopers Hill with a Critical Edition of the Poem* (Berkeley, Calif.), 1969.

[25] Cf. the three in John Ogilby's *Fables*, 2nd ed., 1668, Nos. 28 (p. 67), 37 (p. 88), 45 (p. 109).

compared with a statesman in disgrace (ll. 273–74). But in the
bulk of the poem Denham has clearly expounded any doctrines
which the prospects evoke for him; so the reader would not expect him in this passage to be exclusively emblematic.

Professor O Hehir cannot believe the stag is so loosely connected with the political and historical argument he finds in the
poem. He therefore interprets the hunt as allegory and discovers
it to represent the fall of Charles I. Unhappily for this imaginative design, the royalist poet himself describes the hunt as innocent and happy. The poet also describes the king as leading
the hunt, and finally he describes the king as killing the stag.

I shall not go into the details of Professor O Hehir's argument. He sees at once the obstacles I have pointed out, and he
ingeniously, if not wisely, disposes of them. What he does not
dispose of is this question. If the poet intended the deer to represent the king, why did he explicitly say the king hunted and
killed the deer? Or if he was giving an allegorical account of the
supreme historical tragedy of his lifetime, why did he explicitly
associate it with such epithets as "innocent" and "happy"? Why
did the poet through his explicit remarks throw the reader off
the track of the emblematic meaning? What did he gain? It is
hardly conceivable that a poet should deliver his account of an
event familiar to every possible reader in a form that would
mislead all but the most curious and subtle.

If a scholar chooses to find such meanings in *Coopers Hill*, the
force impelling him must surely be the desire to deepen and
enrich a poem of which Dr. Johnson said, "The digressions are
too long, the morality too frequent, and the sentiments sometimes such as will not bear a rigorous enquiry" (Life of Denham,
par. 29). The way the scholar deepens and enriches it, would
seem, I think, to endow it with the power that Symbolist and
post-Symbolist poets attributed to their images. He tries to

make the poem suggestive and evocative, allegorical and emblematic, in the way that Ezra Pound once hoped his ideograms would be. But in so doing, he has defied and flown from the explicit language of the poet.[26]

Professor O Hehir avoids committing himself unqualifiedly to the interpretation I have summarized. If his argument is bold, his hedges are visible. But Professor Wasserman, in a similar use of allegory, refuses to allow for other interpretations than his own, which he insists is correct in every detail.[27] What I have in mind is fifty-odd lines from Pope's *Windsor Forest*. These lines deal with the nymph Lodona, who belonged to Diana when the goddess lived in Windsor Forest. One day, Pope says, Lodona wandered outside the forest and was seen by Pan, who loved her at once and wished to rape her. Lodona ran to preserve her chastity. But Pan was too fast. So Diana saved the nymph by turning her into the river Loddon.

We are asked to believe that Windsor Forest represents England in a state of harmony, that Lodona represents the English people straying from harmony into the War of the Spanish Succession, and that Pan represents war. Pope himself nowhere says any of this; and he neither echoes nor alludes to another poem that does so. The allegory depends first on the description

[26] Earl Wasserman, in a study to which Professor O Hehir is immensely indebted, first gave the stag hunt an allegorical interpretation; but he decided it represented the trial and death of Lord Strafford (*The Subtler Language* [Baltimore, Md., 1959], pp. 72–76). Ruth Nevo, in *The Dial of Virtue: A Study of Poems on Affairs of State in the Seventeenth Century* (Princeton, 1963), accepted Professor Wasserman's interpretation; but Professor O Hehir has disproved it. I should say frivolously that if the stag hunt must be interpreted as an allegory of the life of a king, the subject is more likely Richard II than Charles I: Richard's badge was a white hart, and he was indeed destroyed by a king.

[27] Wasserman (cited in preceding note), pp. 133–39.

Pope gives of the nymph; next, on her "straying" outside the forest during a hunt; and finally on the character of Pan.

Pope describes Lodona as looking very much like Diana but as scorning both the praise and the care of beauty. Lodona loves hunting; she wears a simple belt around her waist, a fillet around her hair, a quiver on her shoulder. We are asked to believe that in her indifference to her own beauty the nymph reveals a contempt for the principle of order. Since Pope nowhere says this, it must be inferred. Yet the clear language of the passage seems praise of Lodona:

> Scarce could the goddess from her nymph be known,
> But by the crescent and the golden zone,
> She scorn'd the praise of beauty, and the care;
> A belt her waste, a fillet binds her hair,
> A painted quiver on her shoulder sounds,
> And with her dart the flying deer she wounds. (ll. 175–80)

The nymph is as chaste and beautiful as Diana; but (in keeping with a well-known *topos*) hunting means more to her than sexual passion; and she is not vain. This sounds to me like explicit praise. And what are the literary sources of Pope's description, if one seeks possible echoes? The chief sources turn out to be Dryden's descriptions of Venus and Camilla in his translation of the *Aeneid*—hardly censorious allusions, as any reader of them will learn.

Pope says that in her eagerness to hunt the deer, Lodona wandered out of the forest—"Beyond the forest's verdant limits stray'd" (l. 182). We are told that this act suggests a movement out of the realm of order and nature's law, into chaos (p. 137), a movement which in turn suggests the involvement of the English people in the War of the Spanish Succession. Pope mentions neither order nor law nor war nor chaos. So the meaning must be inferred. Now if one leaves the forest, where does one go? Pope explicitly says that beside the forest in his landscape are pasture and tillage (37), fruitful fields (26), Ceres' gifts (39), yellow harvests (88). Are we to suppose the poem, by a movement out of a forest into cultivated fields represents a descent from order into chaos? Why should a poet choose a nymph explicitly associated with cold water and chastity to represent a nation plunging into war?

Professor Wasserman in his account repeats the word "stray'd" as if Pope employed that word in a pejorative sense. But earlier in *Windsor Forest* the poet applies the word to the motion of the goddess Diana herself (l. 165); and in his translation of the *Aeneid* Dryden gives us the original of Pope's expression when Venus appears dressed as a huntress and asks Aeneas and Achates whether they have seen a sister huntress who "in the forest stray'd" (1.445). The word means no more than "wandered," or "roamed."

Pope says Pan saw Lodona, loved her, and "burning with desire" pursued her. We are told that Pan can be identified with disorder and chaotic war (p. 137). Pope says nothing of the sort, only that Pan saw, loved, and pursued the nymph. So any further meaning must be inferred. For his own inference Professor Wasserman turns to Francis Bacon's *De Sapientia Veterum*, but this is a book which Pope is not known to have read. If one looks elsewhere in *Windsor Forest*, one meets Pan as the familiar god of shepherds and pastures, in the famous line, "See Pan with flocks, with fruits Pomona crown'd" (l. 37). And if one searches in Pope's *Pastorals*, composed at the same time as the bulk of *Windsor Forest*, one meets Pan once more, as a pastoral god (Autumn, l. 81). It is possible that a poet would employ the god of shepherds, in contrast with the goddess of hunters, to stand for war; but his reason would have to be remarkable.

If the poem does embody an allegory so much at odds with its explicit meaning, one has the right to ask why the poet should have been so indifferent to the clear meaning of his words. The argument of *Windsor Forest* is neither immoral nor blasphemous nor dangerous to the government in power. Why then did Pope wish to mislead his reader?

I suggest that this allegory may be another flight from explicit meaning, and that the scholar who produced it may wish to discover in Pope a kind of organic form and symbolic evocativeness that is, rightly or wrongly, more often discovered in the poetry of the last hundred and eighty years. In the study of Augustan literature I wonder whether any obstacle is so great as the nineteenth century, which operates like a young surgeon lifting the face of his mother.[28]

Allegorical interpretations, whether or not they seem improbable, must start from the language of a literary work. The critic may give the imagery and actions of a poem symbolic meaning, but he is still limited by the words he finds. There is another method of flying from the explicit meaning of a work without suffering such a limitation. That is to give the work an ironical interpretation. Since the mid-thirties of this century irony has acquired a eulogistic implication that few critics would quarrel with. This implication probably grew out of the effort to recommend both the poetry and the taste of men like Eliot and Pound to an academic audience. The poetry of the Metaphysicals and that of the modernists gave discomfort to readers who associated the lyric with Keats and Shelley. In order to alter taste, critics altered the language of taste; and irony, which had seemed opposed to poetry was soon identified with it.

Originally, it was the rhetorical device of irony that was commended: that is, saying the opposite of what one means, praising

[28] Professor Wasserman has a very different view of what he is doing; see *The Subtler Language*, pp. 3–12.

by blaming. But as I. A. Richards' talented pupil Empson ele-
vated the merits of ambiguity, the concept of irony was broadened to include the state of indecision conveyed ironically by a
speaker who really was not sure on which side of a great moral
issue he stood. Then Kierkegaardian Irony joined the others;
and the Existentialist praise of a fundamentally ironical moral attitude further enriched the concept. At the same time, in a parallel movement, through the analysis of the Jamesian and Con-
radian novel, the idea of an unreliable narrator became more and
more fashionable, until an author who clearly knew what was
happening in his story and obviously regarded some characters
as worse than others began to seem hopelessly incompetent. The
ironic approach to all genres now appears a most efficient
method of rescuing poems or stories that seem sunk in inconsistency or dullness by landing them on a shore where ambiguity,
uncertainty, and amorality are the signs of grace. This approach
is an old one in classical studies, where a great scholar has called
it the "last expedient of a despairing commentator." [29]

The main device of critics so inclined is to show that the narrator or speaker of a story or poem is not only distinct from the
author but the object of the author's contempt. The critic assumes that the author has deliberately chosen, for greater art-
fulness, not to reveal his attitude openly. So the explicit meaning of the work is *a priori* treated as only apparently explicit.
What the author seems to praise, he blames; where he seems
sympathetic, he is really contemptuous. How are we to know
this? The critic says that the author is a well-known genius; his
work is known to be a remarkable achievement. Therefore if its
apparent faults and inconsistencies can be explained on the basis
of an ironical interpretation, that ought to be preferred to a

[29] Hermann Frankel, *Horace* (Oxford, 1957), p. 46, n. 2.

simple interpretation. Where the genius appears to be blundering (says the critic), especially where he seems to recommend a moral judgment that no genius should be expected to hold, we are justified in looking for an ironical interpretation.

For example, Robert Hopkins has decided that in Goldsmith's *Vicar of Wakefield* the protagonist and narrator, Dr. Primrose, is "an object of satire who is both a clergyman and a fortune-hunter, as well as a professor of optimistic platitudes. His complacency is nauseous, and there is a smugness about the Vicar, who is writing his own romance with himself as the hero, who has seen his platitudes vindicated by experience, and who is in effect telling us that he was right all along." [30] Professor Hopkins says that if we take this view of the novel, it is a better work than if we do not.

I have two preliminary comments to make. First, it is not self-evident that if your interpretation makes a literary work sound better than it did before, it is more valid than one that does not. Secondly, the judgment that a work is ironical in mode does not automatically make the work better than a simpler interpretation would make it.

Like the bulk of critics who wish to transform a simple narrator into an object of the author's contemptuous irony, Professor Hopkins gives most of his attention to the proof that the Vicar is such an object. He rarely stops to consider whether the novel as a whole would be improved if we agreed with him. For example, we are told that the Vicar confuses in his speech the terms of commerce or finance and the language of religion, as when the Vicar calls his beloved children "treasures" (pp. 211–12). Now if we agreed that Goldsmith was indeed exposing the narrator's materialism and hypocrisy by putting such meta-

[30] Robert Hopkins, *The True Genius of Oliver Goldsmith* (Baltimore, Md., 1969), p. 208.

phors into his mouth, would we not also have to blame Goldsmith for treating the language of Christ, St. Paul, St. Augus-
tine, and generations of saints and holy priests as hypocritical?
There is nothing in Dr. Primrose's language that is not a commonplace of Christian homiletics. The more ironical Goldsmith's intention was, therefore, the greater his deafness to verbal associations must have been, and the more ignorantly he
must have misled his readers.

Another piece of evidence is the clichés into which Goldsmith's style drops when he represents a particularly sentimental
or absurd action. One must agree with Professor Hopkins that
the style in these scenes is indeed ridden with clichés of sentiment and expression. The difficulty is that it is so elsewhere as
well. If the texture of style shifted radically at the points exhib-
ited, Goldsmith would be the kind of artist that some scholars
would generously like him to be. Unfortunately, it does not. If,
therefore, those scenes are intended to be ironical, how are we
to be sure the others are not as well?

We are assured that the author is condemning the narrator out
of his own mouth when the Vicar delivers prudential opinions
that go ill with the character of a Christian priest—who, it appears, ought to be a martyr to his own benevolence. This may
be so, and I wish it were. But if it is so, what are we to do with
all the other characters in the book, saintly and satanic, who
deliver the same sentiments? Are we to assume that they too are
being riddled with irony?

There is also the problem of the ending. Suppose the reader is
intended to respond with contempt to the character of the hypocritical, avaricious Vicar? Why then did Goldsmith make him as
happy as possible at the end of the novel? Is this the subtlest
stroke of his irony? Or are we to agree that the "happy ending

does not diminish the satire on optimism" (p. 225)? If it does not, the novelist was amazingly indifferent to the language his readers were accustomed to. "I had nothing now on this side of the grave to wish for," says the Vicar at the end: "all my cares were over; my pleasure was unspeakable." If this is the way Goldsmith treats the character we are to reject, he may be subtly ironical, but his power as a novelist must lie in doubt.

One can give the ironic analysis a thin surface of plausibility only by considering the Vicar in isolation from the rest of the persons in the story. There is no doubt that the Vicar is imperfect. He is too trusting, and fails (like Abraham Adams and Squire Allworthy) to see through deceit and hypocrisy; he sometimes commits moral errors for which he reproaches himself (Ch. 13, last par.); he is not strong enough in maintaining his own standards against the wilfulness of his wife and daughters. Besides, although the Vicar is telling his story in the first person, he is sometimes ironical at his own expense and is sometimes the object of humorous dramatic irony by Goldsmith. Above all, the plot of the story and the finest dramatic ironies depend on his concealing from us his knowledge of two facts: first, that Mr. Burchell (who admires his younger daughter Sophia and seems a feckless, impecunious man of feeling), is really Sir William Thornhill, the rich, eccentric philanthropist; secondly, that Mr. Thornhill, Sir William's young nephew and the Vicar's landlord (who also admires Sophia), is a complete villain. In telling his story, the Vicar dwells on the errors that his ignorance led him into; and it is these that produce both the dramatic ironies and the exposure of his weaknesses. But if we observe the man to whom Goldsmith systematically opposes him in the novel—that is, Mr. Wilmot—we shall see that while prudence is in everybody's mouth, there is a difference between the

avarice that would sacrifice all moral considerations to material
gain and the virtue that takes a rational view of what is required
by sublunary bodies.

One of the most startling invocations of the concept of the
ironical speaker is an analysis recently applied to Swift in his
best-known poem, where he apparently speaks of his own career. The last third of *Verses on the Death of Dr. Swift* reads like a
eulogy of the author said to be delivered by an impartial ac-
quaintance. The self-praise is gross at points and is generally
disgusting to the literary palate. Barry Slepian has tried to show
that the contradictions between the claims made for Swift in
these lines and the reality of his writings and public deeds is so
bold that the claims must be ironical: Swift here mocks himself
as one final example of the vanity condemned earlier in the
poem.[31] We are faced, then, with two alternatives: either Swift is
blowing his own horn, or he is sending himself up.[32]

As usual in ironical readings, the critic selects from the poem
and its environment a few elements that seem incompatible.
Like other critics, he then describes the poet as so careful an artist that he could not have ignored such irregularities. And like
other critics, he also assumes that if the passage is ironical, it
will be better poetry than if it is straightforward.

I don't know how one can prove that any remark, including
the present sentence, is not ironical. But I can suggest that an
ironical interpretation creates greater irregularities than it re-
moves. To begin with, the poem was published with notes by

[31] Barry Slepian, "The Ironic Intention of Swift's Verses on His
Own Death," *RES*, N.S., 14 (1963), 249–56.

[32] One supporter of Slepian is Edward Rosenheim; but even Professor Rosenheim points out that "there are certainly observations and sentiments within even the final section of the poem which, whether wistful or savage, must be taken almost literally" (*PQ* [43, 1964], p. 392).

Swift that sound perfectly straightforward and that require a serious interpretation of the lines quoted by Dr. Slepian. The notes are repetitious, vengeful, and cranky; they explicitly puff Swift and his friends; they explicitly damn his enemies; often they are false. We are told that some lines in the text of the poem are false, e.g., l. 460: "He lash'd the vice but spar'd the name" (Slepian, p. 254). Here Dr. Slepian points out that Swift commonly lashed, or attacked, people by name, and did so in this very poem. But it so happens that Swift produces the same degree of error in several footnotes, as when he says, "In Ireland the Dean was not acquainted with one single Lord Spiritual or Temporal" (note to l. 434). This hyperbole is so gross it has the effect of a lie; it would also be pointless as an irony. One may suppose therefore that in both line 460 and this note the heat of rhetoric dissolved the author's sense of proportion; or else one may suppose that what is simplicity in the notes is irony in the text.

Dr. Slepian finds the poem filled with exaggerations—so many, he says, that Swift could not have intended them seriously (p. 254). Now it may indeed be true that all the super-latives, absolutes, and exaggerations of the poem are ironical, but what shall we make of the following passage? It deals with the celebrated pamphlets Dean Swift wrote in opposition to the coinage by an Englishman of halfpence and farthings for the Irish people; and if the ironical reading is right, Swift here is satirizing his own pride in a famous accomplishment:

> The Dean did by his Pen defeat
> An infamous destructive Cheat.
> Taught Fools their Int'rest how to know;
> And gave them Arms to ward the Blow.
> Envy hath own'd it was his doing,

>To save that helpless Land from Ruin,
>While they who at the Steerage stood,
>And reapt the Profit, sought his Blood. (ll. 407–14)

We may believe that in the dozens of lines like these Swift seriously over-praises himself, or else we may agree that he dramatically ridicules himself for being vain.

We are further advised that the style of the poem climbs at points to a sublime or quasi-sublime level that Swift would have repudiated, as in these lines:

>Fair LIBERTY was all his Cry;
>For her he stood prepar'd to die;
>For her he boldly stood alone;
>For her he oft expos'd his own.

According to the ironical reading, the inflation of language here is meant to poke fun at Swift for exemplifying the same vanity that, earlier in the poem, he attributed to all mankind. By this device the poet shows himself to be no exception to the rule (Slepian, p. 256). Dr. Slepian may be right; but if he is, what shall we make of the lines leading up to his quotation and matching it in sonority?

>He follow'd David's Lesson just,
>*In Princes never put thy Trust.*
>And, would you make him truly sower;
>Provoke him with *a slave in Power:*
>The Irish Senate, if you nam'd,
>With what Impatience he declaim'd! (ll. 341–46)

In a note Swift explained, "The Irish Parliament are reduced to the utmost Degree of Slavery, Flattery, Corruption, and Meanness of Spirit" (*Poems*, ed. Williams, II, 566, n.). Is Swift mocking himself in this note or in the passage it explains? Or does he change without warning from seriousness in his contempt for the Irish senate to irony in the lines on liberty that immediately follow that expression? Either way, one can hardly describe his art as consummate. If the ironical reading is wrong, and all three passages are straightforward, one must still blame Swift for acting as his own eulogist. The question is not, as some critics would suggest, which of these alternatives makes Swift out to be the better poet, but which is the most probable.

What Dr. Slepian overlooks is that irony as such is not charming. What charms us is a change from an appearance of earnestness to a reality of wit, signalizing a change from simplicity to irony. In brilliant irony we expect amusing incongruities of language, or plays on words, or sarcastic innuendoes, or comic deflations of rhetoric, or inversions of points of view. In the widely praised early sections of this poem Swift provides all of these:

> In Pope, I cannot read a Line,
> But with a Sigh, I wish it mine:
> When he can in one couplet fix
> More Sense than I can do in Six:
> It gives me such a jealous Fit,
> I cry, Pox take him, and his Wit. (ll. 47–52)

This is humorous, ironical self-deprecation. If Swift had written so well in the last third of his poem, his vanity would not oppress us. If Dr. Slepian is right, Swift ridicules himself in both places but does so with zest and wit at the beginning of the poem, and with neither at the end. He is for mysterious reasons fumbling in the one passage what he has already shown he could do with elegance in the other.

My long tirade against so many works of learning will make

me seem reactionary. I must sound as if I wish to reduce the meaning of poetry to its paraphrasable doctrine, as if I condemn all genetic or psychological study of literature, as if I oppose every allegorical interpretation, every revelation of irony. I have none of these desires. I ask only that critics and scholars square their expositions of an author's meaning with his explicit statements in the poem they criticize. I never object *a priori* to a suggestion that a poet unconsciously rejects what he openly recommends, or that a poet acted in his own life on principles very different from those he embodied in his work. I am always eager to discover the sources of a poet's language or principles. I welcome ironical readings of ironical literature. I realize that doctrine is often the least valuable part of a masterpiece, and that "meaning" is not always explicit.

But I cannot see that origin is the same as meaning, or that any mode of discourse, such as the ironic or the allusive, is good in itself, without regard to the use made of it by an author. I believe that academic critics, in their obsession with coherence and unity—disguised as organic form—have produced a dogma as mischievous as the pseudo-Aristotelian rules. I cannot see that there is any universal process of creative imagination by which poets of all ages go to work, or that the writers I have misnamed Augustan must be shown to exhibit the same properties as Pound and Joyce before they may stand in my pantheon.

If so many excellent scholars have yielded to specious arguments, the cause, I think, is a shell game played with the whole concept of literary meaning. Suppose we consider what an ingenious poet might have in mind when he writes a poem; there is one interpretation of a text. If we ask what a subtle reader might infer from the same poem, we get another interpretation. The conventional associations of the words, independently of author and reader, will supply a third interpretation.

Finally, there are the persons, events, facts to which a text refers; these might be studied by themselves and give us a fourth interpretation. A good deal of Dryden's reading might have been involved in his characterization of Achitophel. A Restoration courtier with a classical education might have found some things in the character of Achitophel that Dryden never thought of. The Biblical and literary associations of the name can be produced without regard to Dryden or a reader of the poem. The historical Earl of Shaftesbury existed in his own right and can as such be brought into the poem. Yet the meaning of the passages in Dryden's poem that deal with Achitophel seem to me limited by what the author might have expected his reader to get, by what the reader might reasonably attribute to the author, by what either might be expected to know of Achitophel or of Shaftesbury, by what the words of the poem are likely to have meant to Dryden and his audience.

If one shifts without noticing from one of my four possibilities to another, the meaning of any poem becomes immense. But is not literary meaning what they have in common, rather than the sum of their separate, unbounded offerings? Surely, what the author might have in mind belongs to the poem only insofar as a reader might be able to get it from the words the author uses and from the references that can be identified. Exceptions leap to mind; the dangers of mechanically applying such a scheme are obvious. But in general it seems a safer guide to me than the assumptions of the scholars whose work I have been criticizing.[33]

[33] Throughout this paper I am indebted to the wisdom, learning, and humanity of Phillip Harth and Oliver Ferguson.

LAWRENCE LIPKING

A History of the Future

ONCE upon a time, you remember, there *was* a history of the future—Eilert Lövborg wrote it, the man with vine leaves in his hair—but Hedda Gabler, a fierce if perhaps not unintelligent critic, burned it, page by page; and ever since we have waited in vain for the reconstructed text to be published. Nevertheless, the idea of a history of the future continues to haunt intellectuals. Indeed, it might be said that an intellectual can be distinguished from a scholar—a Lövborg from a Tesman—precisely by his commitment to the realm of what he cannot know, the yet-to-come. Whole scholarly disciplines— economics, let us say, or anthropology, or linguistics—suddenly take hold of intellectuals (often to the distress of scholars) at the moment when they begin to view the dynamics of social classes, or human cultures, or language, as somehow inevitable; the moment when predictions and promises are made. Who can resist being on the side of the future? Nor can all the wise ironies of the '70's—our hindsight that after all the apocalypse was not at hand, the future did not happen—dispel our prophetic need. Hedda Gabler herself, for all her cynicism, burned Lövborg's manuscript to influence a human destiny; people do such things; though her plan for the future proved to be futile as his. Nor did Marxist dialectic lose its power simply because its syntheses did not come true. We learn, again and again, what Samuel Johnson knew so well: the life of the mind depends on expectation. And the health of a scholarly field, like that of an individual mind, requires some notion of where it may be going.

To speak of the future of the eighteenth century, however, necessarily sounds a note of paradox. Partly, of course, we touch upon a constant awkward fact of historical scholarship, the same fact that subverts titles like "Renaissance News" and "Where are the Middle Ages going?": the past is past. A historian who confuses his recoveries with discoveries, like the producer of a space-age *Hamlet*, is never more than a step from the absurd. But the eighteenth-century future is even more problematical. For on many sides, in recent years, a suspicion, an uneasiness, a faint restlessness has begun to make itself felt: a fear that eighteenth-century studies, having used up so much energy, may be a little *played out*. Where are the new approaches? reviewers ask; the English Institute asks. And the answers are slow in coming. One reads with a chill, in a recent survey of the year's work, that convention and orthodoxy dominate the field, that "the concepts about the eighteenth century that inform nearly all the writings are the commonplaces of currently received opinion." [1] Have we really come to such a pass? Is the eighteenth century now to be regarded, like the structure of the sonnet, or the American frontier, as something essentially *known?*

[1] Robert Rogers and Richard N. Ramsey, "Recent Studies in the Restoration and Eighteenth Century," *SEL*, 12, no. 3 (1972), 590.

The roots of the future lie, of course, in the past; and such questions respond to a historical situation. During most of this century, eighteenth-century studies have been informed by a sense of mission: defending the great authors of the period from the vulgar, familiar Victorian indictment. Swift, Pope, Johnson, etc. (the indictment goes) are satirists who write from the head, not the heart; they lack compassion; they are neoclassicists, prosaic men of reason, not capable of poetry; they tend to be personally eccentric or unwholesome; they do not belong to the highest order; they do not care for nature, or the common man; they are not, in a word, romantic. Here are propositions foolish enough, and powerful enough, to call for an answering crusade. And the fight has been well joined. To right the wrong, eighteenth-century scholars engaged in a prodigious recovery operation. New editions, new manuscript discoveries, helped present the texts in an accurate and flattering light; a new field, the history of ideas, was developed expressly to reconstruct the contexts of eighteenth-century thought; above all, intelligent critics and teachers persuaded a large audience that eighteenth-century literature was worth reading. To be sure, even now the war has not been won. It is still possible for a literate Englishman or American to say without shame—perhaps even with a certain smugness—that he hates Pope (something that only a shameless ass would say about Chaucer, Milton, or Keats). And to choose only one more example, no important English poet seems more neglected by readers today than James Thomson. Yet such instances should not blind us to the fundamental success of modern eighteenth-century studies. Much of the mission has been accomplished; much of the literature has been recovered.

After the first exuberance, however, the success of any mission may bring on a moment of panic. What then, sings Plato's ghost, what then? Now that the eighteenth century has been

rescued from the malice of its enemies, who will protect it from
the complacency of its friends? For complacency, I am afraid, is
the other side of the coin of panic. There is just a grain of truth
to the caricature of the typical eighteenth-century scholar as a
collector: a polite and amusing person, harmlessly addicted to
correct grammar; a connoisseur, perhaps to a fault, of old wines,
old books, old money, and old ideas. Who else, after all, lives so
fully, knows so well, the sweetness of those days Before the
Revolution (1789, or 1798)? Who else is so well qualified to run
the museum of civilization? Yet as that vision fades—as old
wines become collectors' items, too dear to drink, and Xerox
scatters old books about in mass editions—even the collector
must look for something new. What then, sings the ghost of
G. B. Hill, of R. S. Crane, of Geoffrey Tillotson, of Earl
Wasserman, what then?

   Two answers immediately present themselves to such a question; answers that must be paid attention, because (like it or not)
part of the future does belong to them. They might be called the
Whig and Tory answers; or the answers of the radical and conservative establishments; or simply Fashion and Retrenchment.
But however they disagree with one another, on one point, I
think, they should agree: that my formulation of the question
has been decisively misguided. The party of retrenchment, first
of all, will point out how presumptuous, how small-minded, is
the claim that scholarship has fulfilled its mission of making the
eighteenth century *known*. So much, after all, remains to be
known; so much bad scholarship still pollutes the field, so much
good scholarship is still needed. The long-promised editions of
Dryden, Fielding, and Johnson slowly heave into view, but
Defoe, Richardson, Smollett, Burke, and a host of lesser authors
still require definitive modern texts. Large areas of literary history, like periodical writings and narrative poetry, are relatively

unexplored. Nor can one point to more than a handful of important critical books in recent years. Even undoubted masterpieces, by major authors—for instance, Swift's poems, or Johnson's *Rambler*—have yet to be studied in depth.

Moreover, whole new fields begin to open around us even as
we speak of exhaustion; most of all, the multiple fields of interdisciplinary studies. In the past few years, the artificial isolation
of literary studies from other disciplines has started to break
down on every side. Literature and the other arts, literature and
the sciences, English literature and French, German, Russian,
Chinese, literature and history, politics, philosophy, medicine,
theology—the possibilities seem endless. The American Society
for Eighteenth-Century Studies, founded to institutionalize this
meeting of disciplines, is clearly an idea whose time has come.
Nor can anyone deny, I think, that the impulse toward cross-
fertilization (whose introduction caused such revolutionary
growth in eighteenth-century livestock) should improve the
scholarly breed. How can we understand Sterne without Locke?
Thomson without Newton? Fielding without Hogarth? Dryden
without contemporary politics? Johnson without Robert Burton? Diderot without the encyclopedia? The poet Blake without
the artist Blake? The modern divorce between disciplines, unknown to eighteenth-century authors, can be imposed upon
them only at the cost of diminishing their achievement. To
reconstruct the contexts of eighteenth-century thought, to explore and even invent new fields of study, is work enough for
our lifetimes. Surely we do not know too much, but too little.
Surely most of the task of eighteenth-century studies remains to
be done.

This, one need hardly remark, is a sound and useful point of
view. And I myself have so much sympathy for it—and such a
professional stake in it—that only with remorse must I confess

that, looking over the great widening gulf of knowledge, I tend to feel less like Moses on Pisgah, glimpsing the Promised Land, than like Arnold's Empedocles gazing into Etna. All those activities! All that information! Yet what right have they to call themselves part of a *discipline?* Where do we find a *community* of scholars? If, after sounding the immense future of inter-disciplinary studies, one were to list some of the actual titles of this year's articles—"The Microscopic Eye: an anatomy of vision in *musca domestica*"; "The Logical Status of Lillabullero"—the echo might rebound like one of Arnold's niggling gibes; perhaps "Wragg is in custody." For two disciplines, all too often, add up to less than one. The scholar, laboring to master and protect his new expertise, may well find himself turning into a technocrat, whose labors carry him helplessly away from the center of the text; the reader may well cite the law of diminishing returns.

The point is banal, it goes without saying, but let me say it once more. Samuel Johnson knew virtually everything worth knowing in his time: not only poetry, but canon law, aerodynamics, and Portuguese. Unless we know a good deal about Father Lobo and the *Lusiads,* we shall miss significant elements in his work. But the important fact about Johnson, surely, is not that he knew so many things separately, but that he knew them together. He was not so much a collector of facts—collectors did not stand high in his regard—as a user of them; a moralist and critic who required infinite particulars with which to build the tensile strength of his generalizations. And the scholar who knows canon law, or aerodynamics, or Portuguese, or poetry, will not after all have much to tell us about Johnson unless he retains a sense of proportion, a sense of what Johnson is about as a whole. So much is obvious. But it is not obvious that the growth in eighteenth-century studies, or in publications, has contributed a great deal to that sense of proportion. Indeed, much of the scholar's own best instinct, nourished by a healthy skepticism and a tendency to distrust the finer sort of generalization, may work against his grasp of Johnson; and the mere accumulation of details will not help anyone to catch a better likeness. Rather, the proliferation of fields, and of experts in those fields, often seems to obey the laws of its own momentum: so many jobs, minds, pages to be filled. Granted, we need to know much more about the eighteenth century—and given the conditions of the university, the tide of knowledge will continue to swell throughout the foreseeable future. But where are the books that will tell us how to use what we know?

Here, perhaps with a smile of amusement at the innocence of such questions, another party may make itself heard. For why, in any case, should one expect the keepers of knowledge to understand or control their own activities, any more than scientists can be expected, without outside pressure, to control the results of technology? Scholars, left alone, will turn to pedantry; the future is not their business. New approaches to eighteenth-century studies, this argument runs, must come from another source: the needs of society, or intellectual life in general. Who could have predicted, thirty years ago, the resurgence of interest in William Blake? More recently, who could have predicted that the moral of *Clarissa* would soon strike many readers as a matter of urgent personal concern? Certainly not eighteenth-century scholars. The fact is, Blake has become popular because so many ordinary people (not necessarily those who understand him the best) find that he can tell them something important about contemporary life; just as Johnson was recovered, earlier in this century, largely as a stay against modern confusions. Scholars obey fashion or (to put a better face on it) the *Zeitgeist;* they do not originate the needs for knowledge that they satisfy. Similarly, the mainstream of literary criticism, every ten years or so, meanders into a different path, leaving new treasures on the shore: the metaphysical poets; Gerard Manley Hopkins; Christopher Smart. To argue against this process would be as futile as the commands of King Canute (though one need not, of course, go to the McLuhanite extreme of ordering the sea not to stop). It is fruitless to worry that eighteenth-century studies may be played out, fruitless to try to predict what new kinds of relevance the future may toss our way. The job of a scholar or critic, rather, is to listen to society; to be responsive. The history of the future will be written by forces, by human needs, beyond our control.

"Must helpless Man, in Ignorance sedate, / Roll darkling down the Torrent of his Fate?" Of course he must. Nor should the prospect of such a future, as it thrusts itself upon our present, fill us with terror. To be sure, some violence may be done to literary texts as fashion has its way with them: ardent feminists may want to read *Roxana* or *Clarissa*, or to recapture Mrs. Aphra Behn or the Countess of Winchilsea, in ways that a more traditional scholar may not approve; revolutionaries may want to find in Blake, as counter-revolutionaries find in Burke, distorted lineaments of their own gratified desire. But texts profit far more from passionate attention than from indifference. In the long run, we may be confident, the pressure exerted by the needs of society will lead to better readings, even to better editions. Similarly, the current vogue for Gothic fiction is bound to eventuate in a better understanding of the principles of fiction as a whole. Such fashions, such revisions, testify to the continuing vitality of eighteenth-century literature. Moreover, how else can the validity of a new critical approach be tested, but by measuring it against the standards set by works of other ages? Shklovsky's famous article,[2] for instance, not only praises

[2] Viktor Shklovsky, "A Parodying Novel: Sterne's *Tristram Shandy*." The essay dates from 1921; a later version is translated in *Laurence*

Tristram Shandy, by showing how well it obeys the canons of Russian formalism, but helps authenticate Russian formalism, by showing how well it can deal with *Tristram Shandy*. Reciprocal enlightenment like this, the conversion of old to new and new to old, is essential to the health of criticism. Nor need we fear, if we have any confidence in eighteenth-century works, that every new *Zeitgeist* will not find in them something to admire.

Nevertheless, the future, I think, deserves better than this from us. However sensitive to what the age demands, eighteenth-century studies will achieve little unless they remain true to something else: true first of all, of course, to the realities of the period itself; and beyond that, true to the special insights about ourselves, the resistance to modern ways of seeing things, the contradictions of fashion, that eighteenth-century authors promote. A scholarship and criticism built entirely upon putting the past to use will inevitably distort the objects of its vision. Moreover, it may come to prize inchoate, malleable works above more finished achievements. How usable, for instance, is Pope? Johnson's disturbing praise, that Pope had brought versification to its furthest possible improvement—"Art and diligence have now done their best, and what shall be added will be the effort of tedious toil and needless curiosity" [3]—seems at least partly confirmed by T. S. Eliot's unsuccessful attempt, in the first draft of *The Waste Land*, to tap a Popean vein. Are we to hold Pope's success, his perfection, against him? and to prefer that trove for modern poets, the *Jubilate Agno*, on the grounds that Smart himself, fortunately, did not know he had written a poem? Fashion makes strange canons. But eighteenth-century studies can hardly exist unless they resist such canons, and draw

---

Sterne: A Collection of Critical Essays, ed. John Traugott (Englewood Cliffs, N.J., 1968).

[3] *Lives of the English Poets*, ed. G. B. Hill (Oxford, 1905), III, 251.

part of their impetus from *within* the period. Otherwise the
eighteenth century will not be part of the future, but merely a
footnote to it. And worse. Responding belatedly to fashion, constantly balancing conservative, modest scholarship against each
new thrilling call to revolution, scholars may well begin to find
their own work—or even their favorite authors—somehow in-
authentic; a suit of clothes, tailored to each new fashion, that
flaps like a scarecrow in the wind.

Such problems are by no means purely theoretical. Let me
give an example of how the conflict of parties might work in
practice. One subject that does seem to have a future in eighteenth-century studies, whatever we may think of it, is madness.
Folly and the irrational preoccupy the great authors of the
period; they sustain the epic of the age, its *Dunciad*, and lend
Swift and Johnson much of their cutting edge, the nightmares
by which they live. No century has been more haunted by madness; except perhaps our own. Nor has the fascination of
madness lost its power, for all our attempts to regard it as
merely "mental pathology." The subject is as up-to-the-minute,
as forward looking as Thomas Pynchon's latest novel.[4] We
need good studies of eighteenth-century madness; and more
than one, I gather, is under way.

Yet just what is it that we need? Not, certainly, a repetition
of the stale old canard that Swift and Blake (or for that matter
Johnson, Smart, Cowper) are "mad" or represent a "school of
madness"—whatever that might be. The scholar will look for
sounder information. He will define the individual pathology of
certain authors with care, looking for support both to contemporary diagnoses and to modern medicine (much of this work has

[4] The paranoia of *Gravity's Rainbow*, eighteenth-century scholars will
have noted, marks it as an expanded version of *Tale of a Tub*, written
from the point of view of the astronomer in *Rasselas*.

already been done). More important, he will try to put the literature of madness into an eighteenth-century context, one that includes the public shows of Bedlam as well as the enthusiastic fits brought on by religious revivals. He will point to literary predecessors like Burton, and to the ways that the English malady differs from that of other nations. Melancholy, vapors, spleen, the hyps will all receive their sub-chapters. And eventually we shall all know a great deal more than we do now; certified, perhaps, by a new periodical: The Eighteenth-Century Pathology of Mind and Literature Quarterly.

So much for retrenchment. Finally, it seems, the gathering of information might serve to make the literature of madness not so much available as respectable; or bring it to a point at which only the expert would dare, or care, to talk about it. But that point will never be reached. Madness means too much to us, it is too relevant, to be left to the scholars. And another kind of study, it seems to me, will almost inevitably be written in the future (if it has not been written already): a study of eighteenth-century madness in terms of the most advanced modern theories. Let us say (though indeed this reference, like Norman O. Brown's version of eighteenth-century Freudian madness, is slightly dated) in terms of R. D. Laing. Rather than the objective, neutral tone of more cautious scholarship—which tacitly implies, we should not forget, that madness is *tamable*, something that reasonable men can discuss without risk, in privileged detachment—such a study is likely to wear a proud air of commitment. The brutal treatment of the insane in eighteenth-century prisons will be revealed not as a medical aberration but as a logical consequence of the repressiveness, in the name of reason, that permeates eighteenth-century society as a whole. Christopher Smart, no longer viewed as an amusing eccentric with a distinctive, minor poetic talent, may be seen as the key to his age, a liberated singer whose inspiration throws a clear light on the imbalance of those who clamp their spirits into the vise that society calls "health." And western civilization itself, reaching its apogee in the eighteenth century, may be unmasked as a conspiracy against the mad.

Is this the study that we need? Perhaps it is; I do not want to set myself against the future. Yet I must confess that such a project seems to me facile, too easy. My own oversimplifications, of course, account for much of that facility. But the project is compromised still more because, in effect, it has already been written; footnoted, before composition, by all those modern savants who have publicized already not only the terms of the inquiry but its conclusions. What could the prospective author of such a study hope to learn by writing it? Would he not be in danger of reinforcing and dogmatizing his own modern assumptions? or worse yet, congratulating himself on his ability to see *through* the eighteenth century? Such questions lead to others. How can a field, and the men who labor in that field, hope to retain vitality by subjecting themselves to ideas and fashions that arrive from the outside? Will such a study, however glamorous, not end by seeming a little synthetic, a little demoralizing?

What is the alternative? One possibility, it may be, is suggested by a book not yet mentioned: Michel Foucault's *Histoire de la folie* (1961), translated as *Madness and Civilization: A History of Insanity in the Age of Reason* (1965). In many respects the book deserves the notoriety it has attracted. It is supremely confident in its own generalizations, indifferent to the ideas or scholarship of others, radically innocent. Yet it seems to me clearly distinct, on the one side, from the kind of pedantic historicism I have called Retrenchment, and on the other side, from the desperate up-to-the-minuteness I have called Fashion. Foucault does not begin with the assumption that madness constitutes a subject given or already known, which scholarship can bring into relief by heaping it round with facts. Neither, certainly, does he believe that the "undifferentiated experience" of eighteenth-century madness can be put into focus through the lens of the most advanced modern methods of psychiatry and medicine. Rather, he posits, in setting out, an almost total ignorance: an ignorance not only of the "meaning" of unreason, but of the point where one might stand to be able to discuss it. How can one discuss the madness of another era without patronizing it, without circling back to foregone conclusions? That is the problematic center of Foucault's book; the question, involving subject matter and method together, that provides its motivation. And implicit in that question, it seems, is another possibility: that the nature of eighteenth-century madness, explored without preconceptions, might force us to look at new kinds of problems; to reinspect our own ideas, and the sorts of question we ask, in an eighteenth-century light.

With the specific method that Foucault evolved in answer to his question—his "archeology of a silence"—I cannot be concerned here. Nor can his answers easily be imported into contexts different from his own. To speak in French of folly and unreason, of an Age of Reason and an Enlightenment (however ironically), is to speak with a clarity and authority that cannot be reproduced in English—the language of a country where the Age of Reason never happened. Moreover, in one respect at least, Foucault's way of thought seems fundamentally antipathetic to the eighteenth century. It would be difficult to mount a more thorough attack on the assumption shared by the great majority of eighteenth-century men and women, that there are constants in human nature: unchanging principles of psychology, ethics, even taste, that do not vary from one era to another. In

Foucault's history, if I understand him, everything changes; every era of humanity is fundamentally estranged from every other.

Nevertheless, *Madness and Civilization* has proved to be a fruitful book, especially for Foucault himself. The questions that he asked about unreason, the answers that he constructed, turned out to imply a series of other books; indeed, a whole new way of writing history. To define the unspoken assumptions of another age, apparently one must also define one's own assumptions: the structures of thought, mysteriously silent, so pervasive and automatic that few men recognize the need to justify them. Nor can the task of definition be limited to a single field. Foucault has not founded a school, but many of the most interesting continental historians of ideas seem to be asking similar questions; in psychology, for instance, J. H. Van den Berg; in linguistics, Tullio de Mauro; in economics, Louis Dumont.[5] The spirit that informs their work is a willingness to consider the perspectives of past ages as valid as our own, and hence a corrective to our own spots of blindness and silence. And part of the future, I think, belongs to them.

I am not suggesting, however, that future books on madness and English literature should follow Foucault, or that specific recent works, a specific trend of thought, furnish us with a model. Indeed, I am suggesting the opposite: that better models

[5] Van den Berg is best known for his *Metabletica*, translated by H. F. Croes as *The Changing Nature of Man: Introduction to a Historical Psychology* (1961); I have not seen his recent *History of Logic* (1973). De Mauro's recent work includes *Introduzione alla semantica* (Bari, 1970) and *Senso e significato* (Bari, 1971). In a work in progress, Dumont, author of an essay on the caste system, *Homo Hierarchichus* (1967; tr. Mark Sainsbury, Chicago, 1970), describes the breakdown of hierarchical economics between Mandeville and Marx.

for eighteenth-century studies remain to be found. The party of Retrenchment is right, I think, in saying that we do not know enough; the party of Fashion is right to suggest that the accumulation of knowledge can accomplish little without new perspectives, new ideas. But much of the history of the future will be written, I hope, by another party: by historians whose scrupulous investigation of the past is derived, not from specious claims of objectivity, but from the attempt to discover historical theories more true to the past's sense of itself; by biographers who know that every substantial life creates, for the sake of its subject, an original theory of human nature; by critics open to shock, to the ways in which many eighteenth-century works, seemingly so familiar, surprise our expectations, and force a revision in the critical instrument itself; by men and women, in short, who take neither facts nor methods for granted. Let it be called (with proper respect for ignorance) the party of the Unknown.

Do I claim too much, perhaps, for the unknown? One last example may help define the extent of the claim more precisely: the example of literary history. To be able to write a certain kind of literary history—clear; reasonably comprehensive; authoritative without dogma; not too long; firm in its judgments of which authors are major, which minor; sound in its scholarship; relatively uncontroversial—might be said to testify to the health of a field. And George Sherburn's *Restoration and Eighteenth Century*, most of us would agree, satisfies most of those requirements. But Sherburn's survey is twenty-five years old, and in spirit, perhaps, even older; a culmination of that mission of recovery I spoke of earlier. What would a similar literary history look like today—or ten years from now?

Today, we might well assume, one man could not do the job. Certainly the Oxford History of English Literature and the

Sphere History of Literature in the English Language make that assumption. Too many books have been published, too many specialists and sub-specialists have come into being, literary studies are after all too sophisticated, for one man or one book to hold all that would be required under one head. Indeed, the type of recent literary history often seems to be the *Festschrift:* discrete essays held together, not necessarily by a common interest, but by a common act of homage or social bond. Today's literary history is likely to obey no principle but addition; one piece on Swift plus one piece on Pope plus. . . . If in place of one man's view of the eighteenth century, all that endures must be a potpourri administered by a team—the unintegral in full pursuit of the unreadable—then such is the history that we deserve.

We do not, I agree, deserve better. The reason, however, may lie less in the growth of knowledge, or the pettiness of our concerns, than in the increasing difficulty with the notion of literary history itself. A minimal literary history, it might be assumed, should be able to perform more or less effortlessly a number of functions. It should be able to describe the leading forms or genres of the period, their essential characteristics, the course of their development. It should be able to sketch the lives of authors in such a way as to show how their tendencies as individuals, their special gifts or preoccupations, converged with the possibilities open to authors at the time, to make a literary career. It should be able to define the place of literature in society: to tell us what literature was used for, and how it reflected or did not reflect the nature of society as a whole. And it should be able to do all these things, and perhaps supply us with a critical argument or two as well, not necessarily brilliantly or originally (since literary historians must satisfy too many readers to be allowed the luxury of brilliance or originality), but without embarrassment—without embarrassing the author, or reputable scholars, or a general audience. Does that seem too much to expect?

I fear that it does. For in the current state of the literary historian's art, embodied in books, articles, syllabi, anthologies, no strong consensus seems to exist about any of those underlying principles. Let us take them in order. Literary forms or genres in the eighteenth century, first of all, seem among the most controversial of critical topics. Considering how much time critics spend debating questions of genre—is the *Dunciad* mock-epic or mock-heroic? must every satire end with a positive recommendation?—it is remarkable how little they agree. We hardly know how to define our terms well enough to provide a basis for argument. The older teleological view of prose fiction, for instance, which managed to classify all kinds of work, from *Incognita* to *An Island in the Moon*, according to how well or ill they approximated the standards of something called a "novel," or sometimes a "romance," has now mercifully begun to totter; but no creditable rival has appeared to take its place. How does one chart the history of a series that includes *Pilgrim's Progress; Journal of the Plague Year; Gulliver's Travels; Pamela; Jonathan Wild; Rasselas; The Castle of Otranto; A Sentimental Journey: Sense and Sensibility* (and a *provocateur* might add Hogarth's *Marriage à la Mode*, Hume's *Dialogues concerning Natural Religion*, and *The Marriage of Heaven and Hell*)? The better part, surely, would be to consider them a discrete collection of disparate items: so many imaginary voyages, oriental tales, Menippean satires, and the like. But in that case the possibility of a history, with bases for comparison, lines of development, coherent stages, seems virtually to disappear. The literary historian of the future, one may hope, will have firmer principles on which to rely: better definitions of the kinds or modes of prose fiction, better ways of talking about literary form.

Consider, next, the literary historian's bread-and-butter: those capsule biographies, often with facts and dates buried at the bottom of the page, that lend his narrative at least the surface motion of one author passing away, another coming along. What is the present state of literary biography? In appearance, certainly, it fairly bursts with health. The "definitive" recent biographies of Swift, Hogarth, and Richardson, and installments of Boswell and Pope, show that it is still possible for a scholar to master all the given facts, to make the author his "property." The situation does not look quite so encouraging, however, if one applies another criterion. If an intelligent literary friend, someone who had enjoyed reading (for instance) Ericson's *Young Man Luther*, Bate's *John Keats*, or Painter's *Proust*, were to ask me what recent eighteenth-century biography might give him a similar pleasure—the pleasure of extending his sense of human nature, by observing a lifework evolve from the meeting of a unique man with a seminal time and place—I am not sure what I should answer. I might resolve, indeed, to send him back to the *Lives of the Poets*. And if he were to ask me what *popular* biography to read—for example, whether to look at Peter Quennell's recent lives of Pope and Johnson—I should doubtless tell him to save his time. For on this level, the eighteenth-century remains a preserve better suited for common-room gossip or anecdotal fables (Edith Sitwell's *English Eccentrics* is still the masterpiece of the genre) than for serious people interested in serious estimates of other human beings. The literary historian, it seems to me, still awaits better bridges between the "definitive" and the ephemeral; biographies that spend less space enumerating details of bibliography and personality, and more considering the way that writers come into their own.

Finally, what about relations between literature and society? Here, I think, we shall find American scholarship very rich, or very sparse, depending on whether we are interested in social "myths," the ideals embodied in literary forms, or social "realities," the conditions of life as they appear to the mass of men. We are far better equipped to comprehend pastoral than rural life; Stephen Duck as he appeared to Pope than as he appeared to himself; "The Deserted Village" than "The Village" of Crabbe. In this respect (reversing the situation in biography) English scholars have contributed far more than American. Raymond Williams' *The Country and the City*, for instance, conveys a relentless suspicion of convenient literary myths that hardly finds a counterpart on this side of the water. Similarly, the history of ideas, in eighteenth-century studies, has considerably outstripped the history of daily life; or those assumptions, not risen to logical or ideological formulation, that determine not just what a society preaches, but what it is. The literary historian who sets out to describe the Great Chain of Being or the meaning of "nature" will suffer no dearth of materials; but if he tries to describe the life of an ordinary eighteenth-century child or laborer, he may have to spend some years on primary research. A long time will pass, I think, before those chapters that always seem so elusive in literary histories—the summary of the history of an age, somehow supposed to illuminate or provide a background for its literature—cease to be embarrassing.

Very well then, we may logically conclude: the time has come to stop writing literary histories. Yet the logic of that conclusion derives largely from fatigue; a confusion of the unknown with the unknowable. For a sense of how little can be taken for granted need not lead to defeatism in contemplating the future of the past. Indeed, the very range of what cannot yet be defined about the eighteenth century seems to me the mark of its opportunities. A fully developed scholarly tradition that awaits challenge and renewal by critical theory, a body of literature whose terms seem superficially familiar yet deeply strange, may well suggest that the period can be here, as it has long been on the continent, a source of new approaches for literary studies in general.

I do not think that I am claiming too much. Whoever defines the relation between madness and literature in the eighteenth century, when such relations were unprecedentedly rich, will be contributing to a subject not bounded by any period. Whoever succeeds in dealing fairly and intelligently with the full range of eighteenth-century kinds of prose fiction will clarify our views of prose fiction as a whole—and the eighteenth-century scholar, just because he is not tyrannized by the novel, seems more likely than others to achieve that breakthrough. Whoever manages to integrate the quality of an author's life with his work or his times, or satisfies Johnson's demand that a biography tell us a truth about human nature, will help solve an impasse that afflicts most of today's literary biographers—and if such biographies cannot be accomplished for the eighteenth century, when materials are so plentiful and the moral and intellectual choices open to writers so clear, they can probably not be done at all. And what other period offers such radical changes in society, or better approaches to the pact between poets and the forces of change, than the period that begins with Milton and ends with Blake? Nor can anyone be sure, regarding what he does not know, that he knows enough to formulate the right problems. The wisdom of answers, as Socrates teaches, must always yield to the greater wisdom of questions. But when Eilert Lövborg's manuscript, phoenix-like, is published at last, one of its longest chapters—I confidently predict—will deal with the future of the eighteenth century. I hope we can expect it soon.

Penetration and Impenetrability
in *Clarissa*

That was the devilish part of her—this coldness,
this woodenness, something very profound in her,
which he had felt again this morning
talking to her; an impenetrability.
    —Virginia Woolf, Mrs. Dalloway

࿔ "SAY what strange Motive, Goddess! cou'd compel
/ A well-bred *Lord* t'assault a gentle *Belle?*" The questions posed
by *Clarissa* and *The Rape of the Lock* are remarkably similar. What
cultural changes could have occurred in the thirty-odd years between their first publications so that a situation which in one
major work is the object of Olympian poetic satire could in the
second major work be the subject of tragic fictional involvement? What could turn Pope's savage depiction of the social
repression of natural sexual instincts (symbolized in the Cave of
Spleen) into the praise of the necessary repression of sexuality
that characterizes *Clarissa?* What connection is there between the
barren Baron and the loveless Lovelace, between the social imperatives of the poem and the personal imperatives of the novel?

To a certain extent, *Clarissa* continues *The Rape of the Lock* (as
The Rape of the Lock may continue *The Country Wife*), and Pope
seems presciently aware that his poem could not include a solution to the problem he posed in it. No matter how brilliantly in

effect the poem might laugh the real life participants together
(and the Baron was already dead from smallpox the year before
it was published), in the more severe world of the poem
itself, the conflict is not resolved. The battle stops in mid-ges-
ture, resolvable perhaps in the couplet but not on any social or
psychological level. Pope seems to see no narrative device by
which the conflict he so accurately describes can be resolved by
the characters themselves in a way that the reader will recognize
as valid and possible. "Trust the Muse," says Pope, and the
ringing in of that Horatian topos, have-faith-in-the-poem-to-
transfigure-the-story-it-tells, marks the point where Pope's genius ends its search for a form that might more fully express his
new subject matter. *The Rape of the Lock* is aware of the forces of
a newly emerging definition of the inner life that threatens to
change Belinda's world of social banter into the more terrifying
conflicts of the world of Clarissa. But Pope is writing poetry,
not prose, and part of his greatness arises from the collision between his new themes and his old forms. He understands the in-
adequacy of this kind of poetry to express and develop to the
full the ideas about character that fascinate him; in the *Moral
Essays* and *Arbuthnot* he takes his insight even further, moved in
part perhaps by Donne's lyric energies to personalize his own
more public form. Like Swift in the creation of Gulliver, Pope
in the *Moral Essays* and *Arbuthnot* seems poised between a satiric
and a fictional view of character, between character viewed from
the outside, in analogy to painting, with the goal of caricature
and simplification, and character expressed from within,
through an essentially non-visual exploration of the potentials of
inconsistency and uncertainty.

The perception of cultural change may outrun the formal
means at the writer's disposal to express that change. The creation of fictional character seems to arise from a feeling that ear-

lier attitudes toward character are deficient psychologically, and therefore rhetorically, to face the newly perceived problems of self-definition. Seventeenth-century character, with its varied hagiographic, theophrastan, and satiric strands, is essentially character constructed by rhetoric and viewed from without. When such characters are placed on a stage, in the context of others, their rhetorical balance is transformed into psychological self-containment. We may be asked to laugh at the self-containment (Jonson's Morose) or with it (Wycherley's Horner). But even in the triumph of such a character, there is a necessary human loss that is one of the main themes of Restoration comedy. "The satirist satirized" expresses in rhetorical terms the psychological truth embodied in Horner's final rejection of the affection of Margery Pinchwife in order to preserve the myth of his impotence. Style and language become an end in themselves, and the desire to feed one's ego by the control of others unavoidably leads to personal isolation and despair. But, within traditional literary forms, the entrapped satirist or the entrapped satiric character is as far as the author can go. Wycherley's insight is presented with the traditional impersonality of the dramatist. Pope's use of poetry, with its traditions, precedents, and forms, its natural desire to bring the new into the frame of pre-existing order, similarly leads him to the 'solution' of detachment and distance, character viewed once again from the outside. "Trust the Muse," forget the terror beneath, remember instead "the moving toyshop of the heart." In *The Dunciad* Pope returns to the definition of the poet that he seemed to have left behind in *The Rape of the Lock:* the Olympian detached voice, contemplating with equal measure intricacy and grandeur, beauty and foulness, triviality and apocalypse. Strange that a poet who considered himself to be the latest in a line of great poets stretching back to Homer should spend so much of his last years casting and recasting a more complex and more elaborate version of *Mac Flecknoe*. By turning Pope into MacDryden, *The Dunciad* implicitly announces the failure of detached poetic Olympianism, failed perhaps because it never distinguished clearly enough between the vices and virtues of the personal voice in literature, its mixed portion of fragmentation, empathy, and energy. When Pope attacks more and more by name, at a stage in his career when one might expect Horatian detachment, he is stating quite distinctly that the problem is not action, nor institutions, nor faulty generalizations, nor immoral principles; the problem is in individuals, in their weak sense of themselves and in that necessary corollary, the weakness of the written, self-justifying word.[1]

Personal identity is just as vexed a problem in seventeenth- and eighteenth-century philosophy as it is in literature. But the terms of the problem are generally less complex because conflict is not the philosophers' immediate concern. Descartes' elaboration of medieval distinctions between mind and body was a necessary prelude to his theories of perception and knowledge that could also allay a potential religious hostility. Hobbes, Locke, and Hume, in their own ways, similarly recognize that the

---

[1] In *Samuel Richardson and the Eighteenth-Century Puritan Character* (Hamden, Conn., 1972), Cynthia Griffin Wolff attempts to relate Richardson's ideas to still another aspect of seventeenth-century attitudes toward personal identity, the Puritan conception of the self. But she glosses over the difficulty, pointed out by Sacvan Bercovitch, that "precisely because spiritual autobiography highlighted the solitary confrontation between man and his Maker it came to form a powerful countercurrent to Renaissance individualism." Unlike Clarissa, the Puritans desire to escape the willful self: ". . . self-consciousness functions in these writings to erode individuality." (In a review of *The Puritan Experience: Studies in Spiritual Autobiography* by Owen C. Watkins, *SCN* (Spring 1973), p. 1.)

problem of personal identity cannot be separated from general problems of knowledge, and they discuss questions of consciousness, memory, and bodily continuity with sometimes lesser and sometimes greater intensity. But their questions all aim toward decisions about what each considers to be larger matters. They ask 'what is identity in general?' and 'how do we understand the term identity when it appears in other contexts?' They wonder 'what is a person?' and 'how is one person not another person?' Hobbes and Locke, for example, are especially interested in personal identity within society. Hobbes wants to define the limits of individuals so that no man encroaches too much on the next and he therefore seeks to dispense with the unquantifiable and uncontrollable in human nature. His model for the state is a mechanical being, and his model for human nature is a completely socialized being. Unsocialized thoughts, like unsocialized behavior, must be either brought into the frame of society or expunged:

> The secret thoughts of a man run over all things, holy, prophane, clean, obscene, grave, and light, without shame, or blame; which verball discourse cannot do, farther than the Judgement shall approve of the Time, Place, and Persons. An Anatomist, or a Physitian may speak, or write his judgement of unclean things; because it is not to please, but profit: but for another man to write his extravagant, and pleasant fancies of the same, is as if a man, from being tumbled into the dirt, should come and present himselfe before good company.[2]

[2] *Leviathan*, ed. C. B. Macpherson (Harmondsworth, 1968), p. 137. Hobbes later compares madness with drunkenness as similar effects of excessive (anti-social) passion: "For, (I believe) the most sober men, when they walk alone without care and employment of the mind, would be unwilling the vanity and Extravagance of their thoughts at that time should be publiquely seen: which is a confession, that Passions unguided, are for the most part meere Madnesse" (p. 142). We might look

Locke is similarly interested in the social extensions of the self
and defines consciousness in such a way that he can answer the
later questions 'what is a person in law?' and 'how do we determine responsibility for action?' He calls the question of personal
identity a "forensic" one and discusses such problems as the difference between a person drunk and a person sober, a person
sleeping and a person waking.[3] Hobbes and Locke would basically like to purify the definition of personal identity by connecting it only with one's personal responsibility for action
within society: any anti-social or non-social component of personal identity was an aberration. Even though, for example, at
one point Locke seems to anticipate the use of psychiatry in
courts of law, he also assumes that it will not be used to exoner-
ate or explain but to assign reward and punishment with more
precision.

Since Hume is more sensitive to the phenomenology of everyday life than Hobbes and Locke, he does not demand the same
fixity of personal identity. He basically attacks any idea of a
substantial self that remains unchanging through life and experience. Personal identity, he says, is a "grammatical" fiction that
serves to connect the "republic" or "commonwealth" of one's im-
pressions and ideas. Memory is insufficient to provide total continuity because it "does not so much produce as discover personal identity, by shewing us the relation of cause and effect

---

forward here to Gulliver, Roderick Random, Doctor Slop, and the
many other medical men who populate the eighteenth-century novel.

[3] *An Essay Concerning Human Understanding*, ed. John W. Yolton (London, 1965), I, 287–90. Hobbes says dreams "are caused by the dis-
temper of some of the inward parts of the body" (p. 91). and are therefore connected to other unsocializable behavior. Perhaps the same
assumption from a different point of view animates the form of *Pilgrim's
Progress*, "delivered under the Similitude of a DREAM."

among our different perceptions." [4] Hume finds no difficulty in asserting that our perceptions are always our own, never anyone else's, and that we are always ourselves, whether conscious or not, whether we remember or forget. One might expect that Hume would then argue for bodily continuity as the main criterion of personal identity. But he does not take that step, no matter how he may imply it. Hume's attack is better than his explorations. His pages on personal identity tend to refer more to mind than to body, and more to identity than to person. In one of his first references to personal identity in the *Treatise*, Hume remarks that " 'Tis certain that there is no question in philosophy more abstruse than that concerning identity, and the nature of the uniting principle, which constitutes a person." But, in the Appendix to Book I of the *Treatise*, after saying that consciousness seems to come from "reflecting on past perceptions," Hume can go no further: "But all my hopes vanish, when I come to explain the principles, that unite our successive perceptions in our thought or consciousness. I cannot discover any theory, which gives me satisfaction on this head." [5]

[4] *A Treatise of Human Nature*, ed. L. A. Selby-Bigge (Oxford, 1888), pp. 261, 262. Derek Parfit has recently argued that Hume's concept of personal identity could accommodate schizophrenia, brainwashing, and identity crisis, because he seems to allow for discontinuous selves within the same body. "Personal Identity," *Philosophical Review*, 80, no. 1 (January 1971), pp. 3–27. See also in the same issue the responses by Terence Penelhum and Fraser Crowley, with a rejoinder by Parfit.

[5] *Treatise*, pp. 189, 635–36. Perhaps Hume does not pursue the issue because he is unwilling to take the time necessary for a full attack on the Cartesian assumption of the dependence of body on mind: ". . . j'avais déjà connu en moi très clairement que la nature intelligente est distincte de la corporelle, considérant que toute composition témoigne de la dépendance, et que la dépendance est manifestement un défaut . . ." *Discours de la methode*, ed. Geneviève Rodis-Lewis (Paris, 1966), p. 62.

The final pun indicates Hume's real interest. When the first book of the *Treatise* is rewritten as *An Inquiry Concerning Human Understanding*, the discussion of personal identity is essentially dropped. Despite his attack on a static concept of the self, Hume does not want to pursue the discussion of personal identity any further, into, for example, a definition that might combine process with bodily continuity. Like the other philosophers, whatever range of definitions they offer, Hume seems to consider personal identity a point of vantage from which to view the world outside.

By comparison, the novelists deal instead with the anxiety about identity. With Defoe's first-person narratives or Richardson's epistles (which, unlike Pope's, separate correspondents rather than link them), the pressure of self-definition, the pressure on the working out of problems *now*, intensifies both formally and thematically. There can be no invocation of the traditional topoi of superior poetic insight, no turning aside to more pressing philosophical problems, to be asserted as saving solutions. Fiction identifies the mind and the page, making the creation of a book into an act of self-justification; self-expression becomes inextricably linked to personal identity. Pope may not go further because it is within the novel, as defined by Defoe and Richardson, that a new sense of human separateness is best analyzed and explored—all our basic attitudes towards ourselves, our minds, our bodies, and our relationships with other people, especially male-female relationships. In the uncertainties of prose fiction, with its uncertain grasp on the expository and ordered, all the questions have to be asked again and again, formulated and reformulated; they cannot be provisionally locked into some traditional aesthetic form. Neither muse nor machinery nor philosophic system can be trusted to provide a safe literary refuge. Everyone, author and character alike, must tell his own story. As Anna Howe reports to us after Clarissa's death, ". . . it was always a matter of surprise to her that the sex are generally so averse as they are to writing; since the pen, next to the needle, of all employments, is the most proper, and best suited to their geniuses; and this as well for improvement as amusement." [6]

Pen and penetration. Richardson is not usually considered to be a writer who uses figurative language. He is a plain writer: steeped in common speech, unpoetic, unsoaring. But within *Clarissa* repetitions of certain words and their cognates build patterns that contain a force larger than any immediate context. One such word is *penetration*, as used to characterize the wit and understanding of both Clarissa and Lovelace. Another is *impenetrable*, used to describe the barriers put up by both Clarissa and Lovelace. Still another is *prepossession*, frequently used by the Harlowes to characterize what they believe is Clarissa's predilection for Lovelace. Add to these the varieties of will, legal and personal: *good will, ill will,* and *willful. Character*, of course, is yet another, not only the social nature Pope speaks of in *To a*

[6] Samuel Richardson, *Clarissa*, introd. John Butt (London, 1932), IV, 495. Further citations will be included in the text. For a more extended discussion of non-traditional relations between form and narrator, see Braudy, "The Form of the Sentimental Novel," *Novel*, 7, no. 1 (Fall 1973), pp. 5–13. The use of the word "self-justification" brings to mind the printing use of "justify," that is, to bring out to the edge of the page. The OED records such a usage in 1683 and Richardson the printer would certainly have known it. Wolff, in *Samuel Richardson and the Eighteenth-Century Puritan Character*, has an interesting discussion of the passage from diary to autobiography in terms of self-presentation. See especially Ch. 2, "Richardson's Sources." Diderot, in his *Éloge de Richardson* (1761), remarks that when he meets a friend who has been to England, he always asks first if he saw Richardson and then if he saw Hume, perhaps creating an emblem of his own effort to combine the two.

Lady, but the elements of writing as well, the cryptographical form Lovelace uses for his secret letters, his "cursed algebra." All these words have many interrelations, and in this paper I would like to concentrate on *penetration* and *impenetrable*, with an implicit nod at the others, because the poles of penetration and impenetrability express most clearly what I take to be Richardson's main theme: the efforts of individuals to discover and define themselves by their efforts to penetrate, control, and even destroy others, while they remain impenetrable themselves.

Almost everything that happens to Clarissa she perceives to be a diminishment of her freedom. In *Pamela*, the urge toward marriage and children implied a sense of continuity, a commitment to society, an effort to bring Pamela's values to bear upon a corrupt social world and hopefully reform it. In *Clarissa* society has effectively vanished and the battleground is inside the self. Clarissa enters the novel believing that there are timeless social relations that insure her personal security. She quickly finds that her assumptions are untrue and in the process becomes aware of what she had unconsciously assumed. Her own desires, she finds, will be sacrificed to the desires of her father and brother in order to aggrandize the family wealth and perpetuate the family name. The family good is superior to her own. The first threat to the self comes therefore from what had seemed to be the most secure part of Clarissa's life. She has discovered that familial roles and relations will not bear the moral weight she had placed upon them. She first tries to convince her family that she is not subversive. But she is unsuccessful. They lose their legitimacy for her as keepers of value not because they do not understand her position but because they understand too well the point where family and individual values fatally clash; and on this issue Mrs. Harlowe is as much Clarissa's opponent as Mr. Harlowe, or James, or Arabella. But Clarissa's basic value is singleness, as defined by the relations between both men and women and between parents and children. The novel therefore details the process of Clarissa's disappointment with the traditional ways identity has been defined outside the self. Rationality has failed; legal and religious institutions have failed; and finally the family has failed. What then does "I" mean in a world without the traditional contexts of institutional and intellectual order? Clarissa will finally found her personal continuity and substantiality solely upon the purity of her principles—and in such self-definition deny her less certain past selves, her treacherous heart and body, and her fallible need for other people.

Clarissa's primary fear about marriage, and her objection to Solmes, the suitor her family forces upon her, is the loss of identity it entails:

> *Marriage* is a very solemn engagement, enough to make a young creature's heart ache, with the *best* prospects, when she thinks seriously of it! To be given up to a strange man; to be ingrafted into a strange family; to give up her very name, as a mark of her becoming his absolute and dependent property; to be obliged to prefer this strange man, to father, mother—to everybody: and his humours to all her own—or to contend perhaps, in breach of a vowed duty, for every innocent instance of free-will. To go no-whither: to make acquaintance: to give up acquaintance: to renounce even the strictest friendships perhaps; all at his pleasure, whether she thinks it reasonable to do so or not: surely, sir, a young creature ought not to be obliged to make all these sacrifices but for such a man as she can love. If she be, how sad must be the case! How miserable the life, if to be called *life!* [7]

[7] I, 152–53, the copy of a letter from Clarissa to her Uncle John Harlowe that she sends to Anna Howe. Compare Gibbon on Blackstone:

188 · LEO BRAUDY

As the novel makes clear, you must distrust society and the world around you, even your own family and the one you love. They all want to steal your self away, to penetrate your ideas, to prepossess your feelings, to bend your will to their own. The only answer is to trust the principles you find within: "Principles that *are* in my mind; that I *found* there; implanted, no doubt, by the first gracious Planter: which therefore *impel* me, as I may say, to act up to them, that thereby I may, to the best of my judgment, be enabled to comport myself worthily in both states (the single and the married), let others act as they will by *me*" (II, 306). But how is that *me* to be defined?

For Clarissa, as for Lovelace in his own way, the true self is everything that everyone else is not. Self-definition excludes the rest of the world, and, when it does find its values, finds them either in the innate principles of "the first gracious Planter" or in the values of the past. Fred Weinstein and Gerald Platt, in *The Wish to be Free*, have argued that insecurity arises from an attack on contemporary systems of value and the concomitant fear of building a new system of values solely from within. The revolutionary then seeks the sanction of older forms to legitimize his rebellion.[8] As Robespierre reintroduced many feudal and patri-

---

"The matrimonial union is so intimate according to our laws; that the very legal existence of the wife is lost in that of the husband, with whom in general she composes but one person . . . She is however sometimes considered as a separate but inferior being . . ." *The English Essays of Edward Gibbon*, ed. Patricia B. Craddock (Oxford, 1972), pp. 83, 84). See also Christopher Hill's classic article on the social and economic situation, "Clarissa Harlowe and her Times," reprinted many times, perhaps most handily in *Samuel Richardson*, ed. John Carroll (Englewood Cliffs, N. J. 1969), pp. 102–23. Clarissa's metaphorical use of "ingrafted" bears strong resemblance to her invocation of "the first gracious Planter" in the next quotation.

[8] *The Wish to be Free: Society, Psyche, and Value Change* (Berkeley and Los Angeles, 1969), pp. 108–36.

archal values and practices, so Clarissa, whose radical idealism rejects even such primitive social forms, will gradually define herself as an example, an anti-physical saint. And so she is accepted by her admirers, notably Belford, her prime disciple, who writes to Lovelace:

> . . . I have conceived such a profound reverence for her sense and judgment, that, far from thinking the man excusable who should treat her basely, I am ready to regret such an angel of a woman should even marry. She is in my eye all mind: and were she to meet with a man all mind likewise, why should the charming qualities she is mistress of be endangered? Why should such an angel be plunged so low into the vulgar offices of domestic life? Were she mine, I should hardly wish to see her a mother, unless there were a kind of moral certainty that minds like hers could be propagated. For why, in short, should not the work of bodies be left to *mere* bodies? (II, 243–44)

Clarissa explores and helps define the cultural moment when the self-willed isolation of the individual that insures a security against the world becomes first an opposition between self and society and finally a mutually exclusive definition of the images of male and female. Weinstein and Platt have further argued that, with the industrial revolution, the formerly undifferentiated roles of husband and wife—both controlling and both nurturing—separated into the controlling father and the nurturing mother, the one who comes home only to command and the other who stays home, without commanding and with only ameliorative power. This division is already present in Mr. and Mrs. Harlowe: the unapproachable God-like tyrant and the wheedling, sympathetic, and subordinated mother. None of Clarissa's experience in the novel does anything to contradict this definition of male and female roles. In fact, she expands and institutionalizes it—as Belford's remarks indicate—into a general denial of sexuality. Like Richardson when he writes the novel, Clarissa separates herself into masculine and feminine parts and defines them against each other into even greater purity. In search of the anti-masculine self Clarissa desires, Richardson has taken the first step towards the concept of "the opposite sex" and the rigidification of male and female roles that would be the heritage of the nineteenth century and our own.

Pen, penetration, prepossession, impenetrable. Obviously the sexual nuance is there in the abstract language. But, without undervaluing sexuality, I think that its function in *Clarissa* should be seen in a larger context. The fear of sexuality in *Clarissa* constitutes only the most obvious expression of a general fear of relationship and vulnerability that characterizes both Clarissa and Lovelace.[9] Here are two passages, both from the third volume of the novel, and both remarks by Lovelace. In the first, to Belford, Lovelace describes an incident during which he had grabbed Clarissa's hand and implored her to accept him as a lover: "And I snatched her hand, and more than kissed it; I was ready to devour it. There was, I believe, a kind of frenzy in my manner which threw her into a panic like that of Semele perhaps, when the Thunderer, in all his majesty, surrounded with ten thousand celestial burning-glasses, was about to scorch her into a cinder" (II, 98).

The unbowdlerized story, of course, is that Semele desired Zeus to come upon her in all his godhead, undisguised, and that the intercourse itself destroyed her, except for the fertilized

[9] Ian Watt, for example, emphasizes sexuality more exclusively and makes a dichotomy between Clarissa and Lovelace without discussing their similarities. See *The Rise of the Novel* (Berkeley and Los Angeles, 1957), pp. 230–38. On 232, Watts says, "Even so, Clarissa dies; sexual intercourse, apparently, means death for the woman." Here Watt glosses over both Clarissa's will and Lovelace's fears.

germ that would become Dionysus. Whose coyness then is the ten thousand celestial burning-glasses, Richardson's or Lovelace's? It certainly suits with Lovelace's character, for, in its avoidance of the actual myth, it expresses Lovelace's simultaneous desire to assert sexual power and to shrink from that power's destructive potential. His own remark in this situation, as Clarissa has reported it to Anna Howe a few pages earlier, is much more passive: ". . . take me, take me to yourself; mould me as you please; I am wax in your hands; give me your own impression, and seal me for ever yours" (II, 80). How precarious is that self-assertion by which Lovelace defines himself! Precarious in the same way as Clarissa's, for both fear the weakness and vulnerability that they blame on their sexuality. To compensate for his weakness, Lovelace makes his sexuality into a weapon, and Clarissa's refusal of sexuality is the shield she fashions from the same impulses. Because of his disguises, Clarissa calls Lovelace the "perfect Proteus" and insists to Anna Howe that she is not being herself contradictory, but only reporting Lovelace's self-contradictions. Yet Lovelace's uncertainties awaken a "divided soul" in Clarissa as well, and to his changeability she gradually opposes her self-purification. Clarissa becomes clarissima.

Far from being the expression of an abstract, semi-allegorical opposition between flesh and spirit, the relationship between Clarissa and Lovelace develops into a set of polarized self-images because the characters believe those responses are increasingly appropriate to the situations in which they find themselves.[10]

[10] Compare, for example, Alan Wendt's statement that Lovelace is the "appeal of the flesh" to Clarissa, while Clarissa is the "appeal of the spirit" to Lovelace; in "Clarissa's Coffin," *PQ*, 39 (1960), 485. But Lovelace's fear of sexuality is strong—"How does this damned love unman me!" (II, 526)—and he generally avoids any real consummation (IV, 297). See also Gregory Bateson's discussion of "double bind," especially

Clarissa and Lovelace further elaborate the balance-sheet self
that so preoccupied Robinson Crusoe and Pamela, in which
goods and evils, benefits and demerits, were entered in parallel
columns. But identity in *Clarissa* can no longer be the combination or even the choice of one or the other side of the equation.
One must choose absolutely; there is no third term. Using Lovelace to define herself (as he uses her), Clarissa believes that she is
a totally interior being, while he is totally exterior. The true
self, as she defines it, is a purging of the external world—the
theatrical, role-playing definition of identity Lovelace em-
bodies—as well as the divisions he excites within her, her "divided soul." In order to achieve true singularity, there can be no
ambivalence, no past vacillations. Each step along the way to
Clarissa's self-willed death is a sloughing away of the snakeskin
of some past self. In Richardson's profound paradox, Clarissa
believes that her justification will come through the opinion of
others about her inner worth, and she becomes pure to justify
the exemplary view of her others hold. Like so many Enlightenment figures, torn between the desire for autonomy and the anxiety of rejecting traditional standards, Clarissa seeks her justification in the future, from those who will learn from her story
and her example.[11] Samuel Johnson tried to purge some of his
own anxiety about self-assertion by coming as a grown man to
bare his head in the public square of Uttoxeter, there to expiate
a childhood disobedience of his father. But Clarissa turns her
will inward and expresses her self-sufficiency by destroying the
self that dared assert itself.

---

the way two people in a relationship will begin to caricature themselves
each in opposition to the other (in *Steps to an Ecology of Mind* [New York,
1972], especially Part III, "Form and Pathology in Relationship").
   [11] R. D. Laing in *Self and Others* remarks: "To live in the past or in
the future may be less satisfying than to live in the present, but it can
never be as disillusioning" (Harmondsworth 1971), p. 48.

Since physicality is the most obvious barrier to that self-definition, Clarissa turns more and more against her own body. The body, she decides, is the weak barricade before the mind, the will, and ultimately the soul. The eye first allows the breach in that barricade: another's eye, which attempts first to possess one visually, then physically, and finally psychically; or your own eye, which must necessarily be deluded by the specious beauty of external form. As Anna Howe writes to Clarissa, "The eye, my dear, the wicked eye, has such a strict alliance with the heart, and both have such enmity to the understanding! What an unequal union, the mind and body! All the senses, like the family at Harlowe Place, in a confederacy against that which would animate, and give honour to the whole, were it allowed its proper precedence" (II, 116–17). That which would animate is, of course, the anima, the soul. Anna Howe's parallel invokes neither Locke's legal definition of identity, self as the name for the individual acting in society, nor Hume's conglomerate identity, self as the name for all that is you. It implies instead a need to purge oneself of the senses, as Clarissa must purge herself of her family, to gain true self-identity. Passion, Clarissa writes to Anna Howe, is the same in both sexes: "Those passions in our sex which we take no pains to subdue, may have one and the same source with those infinitely blacker passions which we used so often to condemn in the violent and headstrong of the other sex; and which may be only heightened in *them* by *custom*, and their *freer education*. Let us both, my dear, ponder well this thought; look into ourselves, and fear" (II, 236).

Lovelace, too, is preoccupied with the threat to his eyes. He claims that his antagonism toward women, the revenge he seeks, dates from a youthful jilt. But in a more violent passage, he gives a clue to the depths beneath his attack: "How usual a thing is it for women as well as men, without the least remorse, to ensnare, to cage, and torment, and even with burning knitting-needles to put out the eyes of the poor feathered songster . . . which, however, in proportion to its bulk, has more life than themselves (for a bird is all soul), and of consequence has as much feeling as the human creature!" (II, 247). I could here detail the many analogies in *Clarissa* between caged birds and caged human beings or recall Clarissa's remark about the suitability of the pen and the needle to the talents of women. But it is enough to note the importance that both Clarissa and Lovelace give to the eyes.[12] Richardson has in effect transformed a Renaissance trope into a psychological compulsion. Lovelace may owe his existence to the precedent of Wycherley's Horner. But this time lives and not just maidenheads are at stake. Visibility is not a metaphor for sexuality, just as sexuality is not a metaphor for identity. They are interlocked concepts for Richardson, and the general rejection of metaphor by the eighteenth-century novel underlines its search for what might be called a rhetoric of essences rather than surfaces. Clarissa's refusal of physicality parallels the almost non-visual world of Richardson's novel. Were Adam and Eve blind in Eden? Clarissa supposes her story to show first of all that "the eye is a traitor" (II, 313), indicting the treasonous nature of the visual world, that world of otherness, that the frail eye opens us to. The division between mind and body that Descartes developed as an epistemological assumption has in *Clarissa* become an ontological imperative.[13]

[12] One could, of course, also bring to bear Sandor Ferenczi's demonstration of the parallels between blinding and castration, the eye and the testicle. See "On Eye Symbolism," *Sex in Psycho-analysis* (New York, 1956), pp. 228–33.

[13] It is no mistake then that Belford twice identifies Clarissa with Socrates, and, I would say, Socrates as opposed to Christ. The belief in the resurrection of the body constituted the most important difference

What feminine roles are available to Clarissa in her relationship with Lovelace? Possible models are her mother's relation to her father and Anna Howe's to Hickman, the former an abdication to masculine authority and tyranny and the latter a genial subordination in which the woman has the actual control. There is no continuum of relationship between men and women like that which can exist between persons of the same sex.[14] Especially for the woman who wants to exercise her will morally and personally, there seem to be no real alternatives, only either a total acceptance of the myth of male-female relations or a split between mind and body, in which the body is defined as male and therefore rejected. When Clarissa decides to die after she has been raped by Lovelace, he does not understand. Since Clarissa had been drugged and her mind is therefore inviolate, why should his physical violation of her be so important? (Anna Howe makes the same point in IV, 18.) But Clarissa knows the truth of her frailty: *weakness comes from within*. It is not a diabolical imposition from the outside. The mind is its own place—and the body as well. Against Lovelace she defines her will as a totally mental and spiritual entity, not only separate from desire but opposed to it as well. In the process of her self-definition she rejects both memory, the psychological criterion for the continuous self, and body, the physical criterion for the continuous self.

---

between Christianity and the neoplatonism it sought to reject and replace. But even an idealized body is not sufficient for Clarissa. Socrates exemplifies a sense of self that considers its highest end to be a sublimation up the ladder of being to become . . . perhaps a bird, that being made almost entirely of soul that Lovelace aspires to as well. For further discussion of resurrection as a problem in Christian thought, see Terence Penelhum, *Survival and Disembodied Existence* (New York, 1970).

[14] To make himself known to Belinda, the Baron must act in such a way that he totally alienates her. Does the creation of Thalestris require the creation of Sir Plume to do her bidding?

She holds to herself only the timeless assertion of spirit and will. Once again Richardson has psychologized rhetoric. This is no longer the Renaissance topos of the battle of the sexes, the military images of love poetry, but a definite statement about the incompatibility of the masculine and feminine egos, the warfare between their essential self-definitions. Lovelace believes that the mind and body are separate. But Clarissa believes they are connected as well, to the death of the soul, if the taint of the physical goes too far.[15]

With little sense of the historical background or the way their researches had been foreseen by Richardson among many other writers, R. D. Laing and A. Esterson have systematized and thereby made familiar the pattern of family relationships so clearly portrayed in *Clarissa*. Clarissa first seeks to preserve her will inviolate when her family tries to force her to deny her grandfather's bequest. The social and economic pressures felt by the Harlowes are translated into a pressure upon the one member of the family they believe to be the weakest and most tractable, like Cordelia and Cinderella, a younger daughter. The bond of the Harlowes is their anger against a world they believe is about to attack them. By isolating one person and identifying all the family's problems with that person's actions or refusal to act, the rest of the family is saved from insecurity and conflict. Through the example of the Harlowes we can see how the struc-

[15] Both Clarissa and Lovelace are considered to have a "reptile pride," making the usual identification of Lovelace and Satan a little too facile. Satanhood is not an objective symbolization for the literary reader to make, but a psychological observation of impenetrability and recalcitrance. Such similar phrases and images break down the seeming polarities of Clarissa and Lovelace. Watt, for example, makes much of the Lovelace-spider, Clarissa-fly, formula. But Lovelace also characterizes himself as a fly (II, 140). The satanic possibilities of both their prides may be the most recurrent example of this tendency in the novel.

ture of the modern nuclear family may have been insensibly created as a response to otherwise intolerable social and economic realities. Clarissa responds by setting her mind against her body, becoming the spiritual ancestor of the young girls Laing and Esterson describe in *Sanity, Madness, and the Family*. But one aspect of Clarissa's character prevents her from being a case: her assertion of will and freedom, the step outside the garden gate that ends in her death. What is schizophrenia in the younger daughters of weak will described by Laing and Esterson defines itself in Richardson, thanks to the strength of Clarissa's will, as a psychic ideology. Richardson in *Clarissa* could perhaps justifiably consider Clarissa's response to be necessary and appropriate in a new and increasingly anonymous world. In our own time it has become one of the main elements in a self-limiting, self-destructive response to the world around us.[16]

Clarissa's desire to purify her sense of self bears many similarities to Gulliver's. Compressed between the demands of her family on one side, Lovelace on another, and the injunctions and coaxings of Anna Howe on still a third, Clarissa seeks to define herself to the exclusion of all others: purity of self shall become an example to all around her. Here is the point where satiric simplicity and saintly purity can intersect, in the belief that the most accurate vision of human nature involves the successive shedding of complexity and ambivalence so that character may be defined by exclusion rather than inclusion. Faced with the hostile world around her, Clarissa adopts Gulliver's method, separating her personal identity from the contamination of body in search of a definition of character based on inner principles and order. Both consider the body to be a weak defense against

[16] R. D. Laing and A. Esterson, *Sanity, Madness, and the Family* (Harmondsworth, 1970).

the necessary incursions of the world. Gulliver, true to his theatrical ancestors, defines the threat in terms of the violation of
his reputation, not in the "rakish annals" that Lovelace always
worries about, but in the annals of cleanliness. In Book 1 of
Gulliver's Travels he attempts to "vindicate" himself against hypothetical attacks on his excesses, both sexual and scatological.
In the context of Swift's work his overreaction is absurd. But
underneath is a dark dilemma about the nature of the self that
parallels Clarissa's desire to see herself solely as a being of mind
and spirit. Look within and fear; look outside and fear as well.
The mingled impression of caricature and characterization we
receive from *Gulliver's Travels* conveys the way Gulliver stands
between the comic concerns of Restoration drama and the psychological dilemmas of the novel.[17] I use Gulliver here as a foil
to Clarissa because I do not want to consider Clarissa's situation
to be totally that of a woman in a male world. It is also a human
situation, and that is the source of its power.

Lovelace reflects Gulliver's worries over reputation even more
directly. Servants, Clarissa says at one point, are bad nowadays
because they imitate stage servants (IV, 164). That remark is a
small version of the difficulty of Lovelace, who models his character on the stage libertine—Don Juan, Horner, Dorimant—
even though his personal nature does not really fit the role.
Lovelace is less the descendant of these stage figures than their
victim. Like Clarissa, Lovelace puts a great weight on his own
consistency. She attempts to define and regulate her sense of
personal identity by what she believes to be innate principles of
virtue. He attempts to rule his life in accordance with pre-existing literary and theatrical stereotypes—the "rakish annals" he so

[17] Gulliver's worry about reputation is also paralleled by Clarissa's
fear of crowds (III, 436). Defoe gives a realistic dimension to the solitary's fear of others in *A Journal of the Plague Year*.

frequently invokes. Lovelace therefore represents a type of character and a type of human being very important to the history of the novel—the person warped or ruined by his experience of art.[18] In the history of literature, the novel marks a transition in literature from theatrical and satiric definitions of character—character apprehended from without—to fictional character—character apprehended from within. When critics believe that Clarissa is superior to Lovelace because he seeks external approval while she cultivates the inner life, they accept the attack Richardson's fiction seems to make on the role-playing self and embrace the assumption that hidden things are necessarily superior to visible ones. But Clarissa is as enslaved to the moral attitudes of others in her desire to become an example as Lovelace is enslaved to older forms of literary character. In fact both Lovelace and Clarissa act out of fear that they will themselves disintegrate if they do not first annihilate or by dying obviate the existence of others. In their search for wholeness neither will admit the need for others. The myths of survival that animate Robinson Crusoe, Moll Flanders, Gulliver, Lovelace, and Clarissa assert that the only acceptable self is a self-sufficient one. The only way to avoid the control of others is to control yourself. The response therefore to the threat of penetration, whether physical, mental, or spiritual, is to become impenetrable, to become independent by making others dependent upon you.

Whatever the symbiosis of Clarissa and Lovelace, the novel is still Clarissa's. In the early novel, men tend to be the main char-

[18] In later works, however, it is more often women than men who are supposedly affected. Richardson considered Lovelace to be an original creation: "I intend in him a new Character, not confined to usual Rules." Quoted by T. C. Duncan Eaves and Ben D. Kimpel, in *Samuel Richardson* (Oxford, 1971), p. 211.

acters when vocation and society are the main themes. The issue
in such novels is often 'what place in society is suitable to his
merits?' In novels that have a woman for the central character,
the basic question is usually 'how is the self to be realized,
whether society exists or not?' [19] We first can learn about the
relations between men and women in a particular era from
direct statements about masculine and feminine behavior, the
legal situation, and other factual sources. But more important,
more pervasive, and more elusive, is the symbolic situation of
men and women: how do masculine and feminine stand for different aspects of a total individual, whether that individual is actually a man or a woman? how do new myths emerge from old?
what other cultural forces accompany their creation?

Clarissa marks the definite reversal of the classical and medieval psychomachia of temperate man and emotional woman, for
Clarissa's psychic independence and sense of personal identity
are linked directly with her denial of a physical being that has
responded too precipitately to the lure of a man. Belford reports
to Lovelace: "The lady has been giving orders, with great presence of mind, about her body . . ." (IV, 340). And, in the elaborate will she writes toward the end of the novel, Clarissa
declares "I am nobody's," affirming the interpenetrating
relationship of self-possession and self-denial: "In the first place,
I desire that my body may lie unburied three days after my
decease, or till the pleasure of my father be known concerning
it. But the occasion of my death not admitting of doubt, I will
not, on any account, that it be opened; and it is my desire that it
shall not be touched but by those of my own sex" (IV, 416).

Clarissa lasts a year, but the yearly cycle is unrenewed. Without physicality, without sexuality, there are no bodies, no chil-

[19] This distinction reflects that made by Pope in *To a Lady* between
the private nature of women and the public nature of men.

dren, and no continuity. Clarissa's world is a dead end, and the only thing to do is quickly to get out of it. Clarissa has triumphed by reducing her individual human nature to a purified personal identity. As Lovelace says to Belford shortly before her death, ". . . I admire her more than ever; and . . . my love for her is less *personal*, as I may say, more *intellectual*, than ever I thought it could be to woman" (IV, 262). Or, as Belford describes the deathbed of Mrs. Sinclair, with the prostitutes surrounding it: ". . . as much as I admire, and next to adore, a truly virtuous and elegant woman: for to me it is evident, that as a neat and clean woman must be an angel of a creature, so a sluttish one is the impurest animal in nature" (IV, 381). Need I mention that Belford has referred to Swift's Yahoos in the previous sentence? The gulliverian hatred to the body and its messes has Clarissa as its ideologue and Belford as her acolyte. Sydney Shoemaker in *Self-Knowledge and Self-Identity* describes Descartes's argument that "since he could doubt the existence of bodies, but could not doubt the existence of himself, he could not be a body." [20] The bodily continuity that Hume implied was part of the definition of a person is summarily rejected in Clarissa's idea of herself. She has domesticated Descartes (although Richardson would have been upset at the suggestion) to create a self that exists without conflict or change, bound neither to time nor to society, expressing in her own way what Locke called "the sameness of a rational being." [21]

The parameters within which Richardson's characters seek for a firm sense of identity have much to do with the ways in which the English novel subsequently explores characters as well as with the narrative structures that guide that exploration. Novelistic attitudes toward character both reflect and lead the way

[20] *Self-Knowledge and Self-Identity* (Ithaca, N. Y., 1963), p. 17.
[21] *Essay*, I, 281.

people think about themselves and their world. When literature
on all levels of sophistication becomes the primary link between
people, the main bridge between individuals and society, then
self-images will be greatly controlled by literary images. Until
the advent of film, it is the word that structures the self. Any
discussion of penetration and impenetrability in character must
necessarily lead finally to a discussion of the act of writing itself.

The will that Clarissa writes towards the end of the novel
makes clear that it is not will alone which controls one's identity
and relation to others, but will as embodied in writing. Once
again, Clarissa bears comparison to Gulliver: both parallel their
search for personal purity with a search for linguistic purity;
Clarissa as immediate letter writer stands next to Gulliver as
plain-speaking voyager. The work of recent literature most alluded to in *Clarissa* is not actually *Gulliver*, but *A Tale of a Tub*,
and *A Tale of a Tub* not as a religious tract, but as a work about
writing. Language helps one to possess the potentially fragmented self and keep it whole. Pamela itched to write and hid
her writings by sewing them into her petticoats to swathe her
virginity from Mr. B. Clarissa not only protects herself, she also
objectifies and distances herself by writing. Throughout the
early parts of the novel she worries about the pride involved in
being an example. But, as the novel moves on, she gradually ac-
cepts her exemplary status, in great part because of the self-ob-
jectification created by her own writings. The woman with the
pen confronts the man with the penis. Clarissa changes not so
much by Lovelace's attacks on her as she does by the sense of
self-sufficiency and self-enclosure writing has helped to give her.
Whereas Lovelace uses writing as a disguise, Clarissa uses it as
an inward stay—another re-enactment of the competition between the belief that the self is enriched through role-playing
and stylization and the belief that the truly strong self is purified

and sincere. Once again, Clarissa and Lovelace are similar in their sensitivities, if not in their final positions. In volumes one and two of the novel, they have both been established as adroit and polished users of words. Often admired, they are also often attacked by other characters who complain that they use language as wit, to penetrate, even while they remain personally impenetrable. Like Fielding's ideal in *Joseph Andrews*, they cannot be looked into like a simple book, even for a few pages.[22]

What happens when the two impenetrable penetrators meet? In the early pages of the novel they are both optimistic about their ability to use words for their own best ends. They seem to preserve a Hobbesian belief in the humanness of language and its suitability as a medium for explanation and correspondence. Unlike *A Tale of a Tub*, *Clarissa* seems to imply that language can work: letters can be ways to communicate and justify. Swift calls on the violence of satiric language to renovate and revitalize the dead language around him, preventing it from slipping further into non-meaning. Richardson, in his commitment to plainness and clarity, shows a self-consciousness about language, without questioning its basic nature. At the point where self-justification and communication finally conflict, Richardson chooses to explore while Swift is content to mock. The existence of language may imply the existence of society. But it also implies the existence of self-conscious persons.

The problem of linguistic definition and clarification (to found a true science, to establish a workable society, to express basic religious truths) is therefore necessarily tied to the problem of

[22] Clarissa and Lovelace therefore both share Satan's powers of language. But, while Lovelace revels in being Proteus, Clarissa tries to repress such changes. Yet in the process they are both consummate users of language, and, again like Satan, they use their language to enclose themselves still further.

personal identity: the fears about linguistic fragmentation that plague writers like Swift stand kin to the fears of psychic fragmentation and loss of identity that characterize the speaker of *A Tale of a Tub*. Pope's optimism in the 1730's about the poet's ability to reform language parallels his optimism about the new possibilities for human character. Clarissa in her turn implies that prose is the only medium possible for spiritual meaning and promulgates an anti-physical mysticism based not on ineffability but on language. Clarissa's will assigns destinies and meanings to all; and she designs her coffin as well, imposing her own meaning on her life:

> The principal device, neatly etched on a plate of white metal, is a crowned serpent, with its tail in its mouth, forming a ring, the emblem of eternity; and in the circle made by it is this inscription:
>
>
>
> CLARISSA HARLOWE
> April x
> [Then the year]
> AETAT. XIX.
>
>
> For ornaments: at top, an hour-glass winged. At bottom, an urn.
>
> (IV, 257)

The snake with its tail in its mouth, emblem of eternity, but emblem as well of Clarissa's "reptile pride," the unchanging mind, the necessity for impenetrability and self-sufficiency, the rejection of inconsistency and division. As Belford rails shortly afterward, "what wretched creatures are there in the world! What strangely mixed characters! So sensible and so silly at the same time! What a *various*, what a *foolish* creature is man!" (IV, 299). The "infinite variety" so prized by Moll Flanders has become the single-mindedness of Clarissa. Purified language will make up for the fragmented self. The self-sufficiency through writing that Swift mocks in *A Tale of a Tub* becomes Clarissa's mainstay against the fear of self-annihilation. Through the pen the deepest self is both realized and corrected. As Clarissa writes to Anna Howe early in the novel, "I am almost *afraid* to beg of you, and yet I repeatedly *do*, to give way to that charming spirit, whenever it rises to your pen, which smiles, yet goes to the quick of my fault. What patient shall be afraid of a probe in so delicate a hand?" (I, 345).

Richardson in *Clarissa* therefore finally rejects the possibilities of psychological "inconsistency" and change that Pope explored so brilliantly in the *Moral Essays* and *Arbuthnot*. Pope had firm roots in a literary past and had achieved economic self-sufficiency with his translations of the *Iliad* and the *Odyssey*. Even as he saw the shape of culture changing around him, he could explore and criticize those changes as a kind of secure outsider in his society. Richardson was an insecure insider, a figure of the new world, part aesthete and part businessman. In a period of rapid social and economic change, he perceived the sympathy his audience would feel for characters who needed to maintain a strict hold on the essentials of self, to deny vulnerability, to become impenetrable, at the same time that they insured their self-sufficiency by penetrating and hopefully puncturing everyone who came near enough to threaten the fragile sense of personal identity that lay within them. Self-sufficiency and self-creation is the general message of the novel, and Richardson spoke to a world ready for that message. Clarissa's desire for self-containment closely resembles the personal rigidity of Samuel Johnson, his fear of sloth, his need to purge himself of fault and his works of personality. To speak a *Rambler*, as Mrs. Thrale tells us Johnson could do on request, reflects the same subordination of self to work that Sterne worries in another way, by recognizing the form that self can project rather than fighting against it.

Through Clarissa's rejection of the body, the devil within, and society, the devils without, Richardson articulated better than any writer of his time a group of attitudes toward personal identity and relations with other people that still influence us. Perhaps in our time we can finally cease to believe in those devils and continue Pope's exploration of the values of inconsistency and ambivalence. After all, as we can now see, Freud did not begin a new age. He was the prelude to the end of the old one—an age that the genius of Richardson helps us to define in all its literary fruitfulness and its psychic barrenness.[23]

[23] This essay has benefited greatly from discussions with Sacvan Bercovitch and Richard Kuhns.

THE PROGRAM

I. New Approaches to Eighteenth-Century Literature
   Directed by Lawrence Lipking, Princeton University
   Sat.   11:00 A.M.   A History of the Future
                       Lawrence Lipking, Princeton University
   Sat.   3:15 P.M.   Thinking in Forms
                       Ralph Cohen, University of Virginia
   Sun.   1:45 P.M.   Penetration and Impenetrability in
                       Clarissa
                       Leo Braudy, Columbia University
   Sun.   3:15 P.M.   Recent Philosophy of Mind and
                       Eighteenth-Century Aesthetics
                       William Youngren, Boston College

II. Poets on Poets
    Directed by Theodore Weiss, Princeton University
    Sat.   1:45 P.M.   Marianne Moore
                       Elizabeth Bishop, Harvard University
    Sun.   9:30 A.M.   Dante's *Paradiso*
                       *Howard Nemerov, Washington Univer-
                       sity, St. Louis*
    Sun.   11:00 A.M. Lucretius
                       Theodore Weiss, Princeton University

III. The Emerson Controversy
     Directed by Sacvan Bercovitch, Columbia University
     Mon.   9:30 A.M.   The Freshness of Transformation:
                        Emerson's Dialectics of Influence
                        Harold Bloom, Yale University

Mon. 11:00 A.M.   Ralph Waldo Emerson: The Circles
                    of the Eye
                    James Cox, Dartmouth College
Tues. 9:30 A.M.   Emerson and the Christian Imagina-
                    tion
                    Stephen Donadio, Columbia University
Tues. 11:00 A.M.   Emerson and the Imperial Self: A
                    European Critique
                    Maurice Gonnaud, University of Lyons

IV. Literature of Politics
     Directed by Thomas R. Edwards, Rutgers University
     Mon. 1:45 P.M.   Politics and the Form of Disenchant-
                        ment
                        George L. Levine, Livingston College,
                        Rutgers University
     Mon. 3:15 P.M.   Criticism—and Self-Criticism
                        Lillian S. Robinson, State University of
                        New York at Buffalo
     Tues. 1:45 P.M.   The Radical Romance: *La Chartreuse*
                        de Parme and *Wuthering Heights*
                        Michael Wood, Columbia University
     Tues. 3:15 P.M.   Gentlemen of Principle, Priests of
                        Presumption
                        Benjamin DeMott, Amherst College

Maurianne S. Adams, University of Massachusetts; Ruth M. Adams, Dartmouth College; Gellert S. Alleman, Rutgers University at Newark; Gay Wilson Allen, New York University; Quentin Anderson, Columbia University; Jonathan Arac, Princeton University; Alberta Arthurs, Radcliffe College

George W. Bahlke, Kirkland College; Ashur Baizer, Ithaca College; C. L. Barber, University of California at Santa Cruz; Dorothy K. Barber, University of Minnesota; Laird H. Barber, University of Minnesota; James E. Barcus, Houghton College; Jonas Barish, University of California at Berkeley; Caroline King Barnard, Fairleigh Dickinson University; Warner J. Barnes, University of Texas at Austin; J. Robert Barth, s.j., Harvard University; Bertrice Bartlett, Stephens College; John E. Becker, Fairleigh Dickinson University; Alice R. Bensen, Eastern Michigan University; Sacvan Bercovitch, Columbia University; David E. Berndt, Boston University; Warner Berthoff, Harvard University; J. Thomas Bertrand, U.S. Naval Academy; Frank Bidart, Cambridge, Massachusetts; Murray Biggs, Massachusetts Institute of Technology; Elizabeth Bishop, Harvard University; Susan Blake, University of Connecticut; Sophia B. Blaydes, West Virginia University; Harold Bloom, Yale University; Morton W. Bloomfield, Harvard University; Charles Blyth, Cambridge, Massachusetts; J. P. Boatman, U.S. Naval Academy; Philip Bordinat, West Virginia University; George Bornstein, University of Michigan; John D. Boyd, s.j., Fordham University; Leo Braudy, Columbia University; Susan H. Brisman, Vassar College; Reuben A. Brower, Harvard University; Donna Brown, University of New Hampshire; Judith Gwyn Brown, New York, New York; Warren Brown, University of New Hampshire; Jerome H. Buckley, Harvard University; Lawrence I. Buell, Oberlin College; James Bunn, State University of New York at Buffalo; Sister M. Vincentia Burns, Albertus Magnus College; Roland Burns, University of Maine; Francelia Butler, University of Connecticut

Ruth A. Cameron, Eastern Nazarene College; Margaret Mooney Cana-
van, College of New Rochelle; Thomas R. Carper, University of Maine
at Portland-Gorham; Robert L. Caserio, State University of New York
at Buffalo; David Cavitch, Tufts University; Thomas H. Chalfant,
Alabama State University; Mrs. Peter Chapman, Short Hills, New Jer-
sey; Howell D. Chickering, Jr., Amherst College; John A. Christie,
Vassar College; Ralph A. Ciancio, Skidmore College; Edward D.
Clark, Sr., Fayetteville State University; Sister Mary Cleophas, Loyola
College; James L. Clifford, Columbia University; Ralph Cohen, University of Virginia; Arthur N. Collins, State University of New York
at Albany; David B. Comer III, Georgia Institute of Technology; Phi-
lip Cooper, University of Maryland, Baltimore County; James Cox,
Dartmouth College; Patricia Craddock, Boston University; G. Armour
Craig, Amherst College; Ruth Cunningham, Kenwood Academy

Robert Gorham Davis, Columbia University; Stuart A. Davis, Herbert
Lehman College, CUNY; Winifred M. Davis, Columbia University;
Paul De Man, Yale University; Benjamin De Mott, Amherst College;
Joanne Thérèse Dempsey, Harvard University; Joanne Feit Diehl, Yale
University; Thomas F. Dillingham, Stephens College; Evelyn C.
Dodge, Framingham State College; Muriel Dollar, Caldwell College;
Stephen L. Donadio, Columbia University; E. Talbot Donaldson, Uni-
versity of Michigan; Sister Rose Bernard Donna, c.s.j., The College of
Saint Rose

Dwight Eddins, University of Alabama; Thomas R. Edwards, Rutgers
University; Ronald Ein, Clarkson College of Technology; Frances El-
dredge, Chatham College; David A. Ellis, Tufts University; Martha
Winburn England, Queens College, CUNY; Clyde A. Enroth, Califor-
nia State University at Sacramento; Theresa L. Enroth, American
River College; David V. Erdman, State University of New York at
Stony Brook and New York Public Library; Sister Marie Eugénie, Im-
maculata College

Irene R. Fairley, Northeastern University; N. N. Feltes, York University; Arthur Fenner, University of Detroit; Alfred R. Ferguson, University of Massachusetts at Boston; Frances C. Ferguson, The Johns
Hopkins University; David Ferry, Wellesley College; Philip Fisher,
Brandeis University; John S. Flagg, Suffolk University; Francis Flem-

ing, Salisbury State College; George H. Ford, University of Rochester; Leslie D. Foster, Northern Michigan University; Robert Foulke, Skidmore College; Richard Lee Francis, Western Washington State College; Warren G. French, Indiana-Purdue University at Indianapolis; Albert B. Friedman, Claremont Graduate School; Northrop Frye, Massey College, University of Toronto; Margaretta Fulton, Harvard University Press

Margaret Gage, The Nichols School; Harry R. Garvin, Bucknell University; Marilyn Gaull, Temple University; Blanche H. Gelfant, Dartmouth College; Carol Gesner, Berea College; Jessie A. Gilmer, Staten Island Community College, CUNY; Harold W. Gleason, Jr., Shippensburg State College; Morris Golden, University of Massachusetts; Maurice J. Gonnaud, University Lyon II, France; Stephen H. Good, Mount Saint Mary's College; Gerald T. Gordon, University of Maine; Michael T. Gosman, The Catholic University of America; Sister Mary Eugene Gotimer, College of Mount St. Vincent; Terry H. Grabar, Fitchburg State College; James Gray, Dalhousie University; Mary Elizabeth Green, Arizona State University; John C. Guilds, University of South Carolina; Allen Guttmann, Amherst College

Margaret R. Hale, University of Connecticut; Sarah C. Hall, Polytechnic School; Robert G. Hallwachs, Drexel University; Richard Harrier, New York University; Victor Harris, Brandeis University; Phillip Harth, University of Wisconsin; Geoffrey Hartman, Yale University; Joan E. Hartman, Staten Island Community College, CUNY; E. Ruth Harvey, Victoria College, University of Toronto; Britton J. Harwood, Miami University; Harrison Hayford, Northwestern University; Sister Jean Hemmer, College of Saint Elizabeth; Suzette A. Henke, University of Virginia; Rev. William B. Hill, s.j., University of Scranton; Charles H. Hinnant, University of Missouri; E. D. Hirsch, Jr., University of Virginia; Daniel Hoffman, Library of Congress; Laurence B. Holland, The Johns Hopkins University; Frank S. Hook, Lehigh University; Vivian C. Hopkins, State University of New York at Albany; Susan R. Horton, University of Massachusetts at Boston; Chaviva M. Hošek, Victoria College, University of Toronto; Elizabeth Huberman, Newark State College at Union; Jean M. Humez, Boston University; Samuel Hynes, Northwestern University

John Iorio, University of South Florida; Helen Irvin, Transylvania College

Nora Crow Jaffe, Smith College; Richard Johnson, Mount Holyoke College; Robert P. Kalmey, Shippensburg State College; M. Enamul Karim, Rockford College; Marjorie Kaufman, Mount Holyoke College; Carol Kay, Princeton University; John R. Kayser, University of New Hampshire; Hugh T. Keenan, Georgia State University; Walter B. Kelly, Mary Washington College of the University of Virginia; Rudolf Kirk, Rutgers University; Peter William Koenig, Oakton College; James Kraft, National Endowment for the Humanities; Peggy D. Kraus, American River College

J. Craig La Drière, Harvard University; Mary M. Lago, University of Missouri; Jon Lanham, University of Toronto; Jon S. Lawry, Sudbury, Ontario, Canada; Lewis Leary, The University of North Carolina at Chapel Hill; J. C. Levenson, University of Virginia; George Levine, Livingston College, Rutgers University; Lawrence Lipking, Princeton University; A. Walton Litz, Princeton University; Joseph Paul Lovering, Canisius College; Sister Alice Lubin, College of Saint Elizabeth; Thomas E. Lucas, Seton Hall University

Elizabeth MacAndrew, Cleveland State University; Isabel G. Mac-Caffrey, Harvard University; Muriel McClanahan, George Washington University; Marjorie W. McCune, Susquehanna University; Lucy S. McDiarmid, Boston University; Stuart Y. McDougal, University of Michigan; Fred R. MacFadden, Coppin State College; Thomas Mc-Farland, CUNY Graduate Center; Terence J. McKenzie, U.S. Coast Guard Academy; Paul A. Magnuson, University of Pennsylvania; Daniel Marder, University of Tulsa; Vida E. Marković, University of Belgrade, Yugoslavia; Emerson R. Marks, University of Massachusetts at Boston; Mary G. Mason, Emmanuel College; Donald C. Mell, Jr., University of Delaware; John H. Middendorf, Columbia University; Charles W. Mignon, University of Nebraska; J. Hillis Miller, Yale University; Verne D. Morey, University of Maine at Fort Kent; Julian Moynahan, Rutgers University; David James Murray, University of Nottingham, England

Rae Ann Nager, Harvard University; G. Alan Nelson, Middlesex School; Lowry Nelson, Jr., Yale University; Howard Nemerov, Washington University; John M. Nesselhof, Wells College; Donald R. Noble, University of Alabama; Rev. William T. Noon, s.j., Le Moyne College; Lawrence Noriega, Sweet Briar College

Robert O'Clair, Manhattanville College; Richard Ohmann, Wesleyan University; Nadine Ollman, Drew University; Carol Orr, Princeton University Press; James M. Osborn, Yale University; Charles A. Owen, Jr., University of Connecticut; Lucy Owen, University of Virginia

Roy Harvey Pearce, University of California at San Diego; Norman Holmes Pearson, Yale University; Carl A. Peterson, Oberlin College; Henry H. Peyton III, Memphis State University; William Phillips, Rutgers University; Joel Porte, Harvard University; Robert O. Preyer, Heidelberg University

William Ernest Ray, Memphis State University; Joan Reardon, Barat College; Robert Reid, University of Connecticut; Donald H. Reiman, The Carl H. Pforzheimer Library; Joseph Reino, Villanova University; Louis A. Renza, Dartmouth College; Keith N. Richwine, Western Maryland College; Harriet N. Ritvo, Harvard University; Bruce Robbins, Harvard University; John R. Roberts, University of Missouri; Lillian S. Robinson, State University of New York at Buffalo; P. W. Rogers, Queen's University, Canada; J. Carter Rowland, State University College, Fredonia; Hans H. Rudnick, Southern Illinois University; Rebecca D. Ruggles, Brooklyn College, CUNY; Donald D. Russ, Georgia Institute of Technology; Robert C. Ryan, Boston University

Phillips Salman, Cleveland State University; Irene Samuel, Hunter College, CUNY; Helene B. M. Schnabel, New York, New York; Manuel Schonhorn, Southern Illinois University at Carbondale; H. T. Schultz, Dartmouth College; Richard J. Sexton, Fordham University; Patricia L. Sharde, Smith College; Marc Shell, Yale University; Joan R. Sherman, Rutgers University; William H. Sievert, Pace University; C. Anderson Silber, Victoria College, University of Toronto; John E. Sitter, University of Massachusetts at Amherst; Carol H. Smith, Douglass College, Rutgers University; Marcel Smith, University of Alabama; Rowland Smith, Dalhousie University; Sarah Smith, Cambridge, Massachusetts; Susan Sutton Smith, State University of New

York at Oneonta; Mark Spilka, Brown University; Robert E. Spiller, University of Pennsylvania; Emily B. Stanley, University of Connecticut at Hartford; Susan Staves, Brandeis University; Peter B. Steese, State University College; Edna L. Steeves, University of Rhode Island; A. Wilbur Stevens, University of Nevada; Holly Stevens, Yale University; Albert Stone, Jr., Hellenic College; Floyd C. Stuart, Norwich University; Marcia Stubbs, Wellesley College; Jean Sudrann, Mount Holyoke College; Maureen Sullivan, University of Pennsylvania; U. T. Summers, Rochester Institute of Technology; Donald R. Swanson, Wright State University

Stephen E. Tabachnick, University of the Negev, Beersheba, Israel; Marian Connor Tarbox, Roxbury Community College; Edward W. Tayler, Columbia University; Nathaniel Teich, University of Oregon; Robert D. Thornton, State University of New York at New Paltz; Nancy Tischler, Pennsylvania State University; Robert Tisdale, Carleton College; David O. Tomlinson, U.S. Naval Academy; Margaret Tongue, Salisbury State College; Henry S. Traeger, New York, New York; Lewis A. Turlish, Bates College

Virginia Walker Valentine, University of South Florida; Rosemary T. Van Arsdel, University of Puget Sound; William D. Vanech, Brown University; Helen Vendler, Boston University; Howard P. Vincent, Kent State University

Willis Wager, Boston University; Hyatt H. Waggoner, Brown University; Eugene M. Waith, Yale University; Emily M. Wallace, Philadelphia, Pennsylvania; Elizabeth Walsh, r.s.c.j., Harvard University; Aileen Ward, Brandeis University; Susan Ward, University of Connecticut; Francis W. Warlow, Dickinson College; Herbert Weil, University of Connecticut; Sister Mary Anthony Weinig, Rosemont College; Theodore Weiss, Princeton University; J. K. Welcher, C. W. Post College; René Wellek, Yale University; Ronald C. Wendling, St. Joseph's College; Ruth Whitman, Radcliffe Institute; Joseph Wiesenfarth, University of Wisconsin; Samuel F. Will, Jr., University of Massachusetts; Maurita Willett, University of Illinois; Helen B. Wils, American River College; Kenneth Jay Wilson, University of Rochester; W. K. Wimsatt, Yale University; Calhoun Winton, University of

South Carolina; Michael Wood, Columbia University; Mildred G. Worthington, Bentley College

Sister Donez Xiques, C.N.D., Brooklyn College, CUNY

Donald Yannella, Glassboro State College; Ruth Yeazell, Boston University; William H. Youngren, Boston College